1 MONTH OF
FREE
READING

at
www.ForgottenBooks.com

By purchasing this book you are eligible for one month membership to ForgottenBooks.com, giving you unlimited access to our entire collection of over 1,000,000 titles via our web site and mobile apps.

To claim your free month visit:

www.forgottenbooks.com/free973451

ISBN 978-0-260-81856-0
PIBN 10973451

The Black and Gold

Published by the Upper Classes of the Richard J. Reynolds High School, Winston-Salem, N. C.

VOL. XIII   JUNE, 1924   No. 4

DEDICATION

To Miss Ione Mebane

In appreciation of her loyalty to W. H. S.,

her influence for good felt by every

student and her splendid

RICHARD J. REYNOLDS MEMORIAL AUDITORIUM

A Memorial

THE RICHARD J. REYNOLDS AUDITORIUM

It stands on the hills west of our city, between what is best of the old and what will be beautiful in the new. More than granite and stone, it is less a building than a giant echo flung from a time when thought was so new that men found need to build physical counterparts of what seemed great in their minds. In a city where the labor of men's hands has responded to the imperious foresight of a great workman and builder, there is now a place where the children of these builders may go. There, by means of drama and music, they will learn to use the tools of knowledge, and by so doing, will turn their best thought into contributions to civilization. The student of mathematics may use his knowledge of lines and angles in the erection of other great buildings; perhaps some may be found who will fashion words into memorable pictures of life. From the shadows of this proscenium a great symphony may go forth. All this will come, must come, in time from youth daily confronted by the facade of this memorial. The people have taken it for their own; they have accepted it in a moment made solemn by its dedication to God; they have learned the use of it by assembling there to hear great music. Thinking of it, they will not erect other buildings unworthy of its greatness.

—E. W.

ALICE EVELYN MORRIS

"Ebby" "Rosy"

*"But they whom truth and wisdom lead,
Can gather honey from a weed."*

President Senior Class; Chairman Executive Committee; Assistant Cheer Leader Rooters' Club; Assistant Manager Basketball; Member Twentieth Century Club, Hiking Club, Athletic Association.

GUY RAYMOND FULP

"Ray"

*"A merry heart maketh a cheery
countenance."*

Secretary La Cercle Francaise; Member Calvin H. Wiley Literary Society, Athletic Association.

ADELA DILLARD SHEPPARD

"Pet"

*"Come and trip it as you go, on the
light fantastic toe."*

Captain Varsity Basketball; President Rooters' Club; Member La Cercle Francaise, Twentieth Century Thinkers' Club, Athletic Association.

PAUL HOLCOMB MURPHY

"Gazoopy"

"Bless thee, Virgil; thou are translated."

Chairman Bulletin Board and Magazine Committee Societas Litterarum; Secretary and Treasurer Senior Scientific Club; Member Calvin H. Wiley Literary Society, Athletic Association.

MARY ALAYSIA ACKERMAN

"Bobby" "Murry"

"Forward and frolicsome glee was there,
The will to do, the soul to dare."

Member Rooters' Club, World Events Club, Hiking Club, Athletic Association.

DANIEL JULIUS LUCKENBACH

"Dan"

"He was a gentleman sincere, gracious and renowned."

Executive Committee Senior Class; Library Page (first semester); Senior Football Team; Vice-President Societas Litterarum (first term); President Senior Scientific Club; Member Hi-Y Club, Calvin H. Wiley Literary Society, Orchestra, Band, Athletic Association.

HELEN HAZEL HAUSER

"Nut"

"A day in April never came so sweet."

Executive Committee Senior Class; Press Reporter Senior Class; Class Historian; Library Page; Member La Cercle Francaise, Twentieth Century Thinkers' Club, Rooters' Club, Hiking Club, Athletic Association.

ROBERT IRVIN BARTON

"Chick", "Abie," "Bob"

"Great thoughts like great people need no trumpet."

Vote Committee; Chairman Bulletin Board Committee World Events Club; Member Calvin H. Wiley Literary Society, Spanish Club, Senior Hi-Y Club, Band, Orchestra, Athletic Association.

JENNIE FLORENCE LASLEY

"Jinks"

"Mannerly modesty is the height of virtue."

Library Page; Member Rooters' Club, Hiking Club, La Cercle Francaise, Athletic Association.

ROBERT FRANKLIN FOLTZ

"Bob"

" 'Tis the silent who learn the most and live the longest."

Associate Editor Black and Gold; Library Page; Senior Football Team; Senior Baseball Team; Member Calvin H. Wiley Literary Society, Societas Litterarum, Band, Orchestra, Glee Club, Athletic Association.

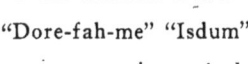

DORE KERNER DAVIS

"Dore-fah-me" "Isdum"

"It's the songs ye sing an' the smiles ye wear, that's making the sun shine everywhere."

Class Poet; Associate Editor Black and Gold; Press Reporter La Cercle Francaise; Member Rooters' Club, Hiking Club, Athletic Association.

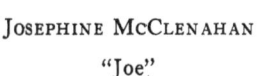

JOSEPHINE McCLENAHAN

"Joe"

"The laughter of girls is and ever was among the delightful sounds of earth."

Senior Baseball Team; Member Spanish Club, Hiking Club, World Events Club, Athletic Association.

RALPH IRVIN CHOPLIN

"Chop"

*"He was not merely a chip of the Block,
but the old Block itself."*

Class Prophet; Typewriting Team;
Alternate Debating Team; Sergeant-at
arms Spanish Club; Secretary World
Events Club (first semester); Member
Hi-Y Club.

ANNIE BELLE PEDDYCORD

"Peddy" "Ann"

"Honor is the reward of virtue."

Library Page; Member La Cercle
Francaise, Twentieth Century Think-
ers' Club, Hiking Club, Rooters' Club,
Athletic Association.

CURTIS CAMERON LANE

"Trick"

*"Intellect is the soul of man, the only
immortal part of him."*

Secretary Societas Litterarum (second
term); Senior Baseball Team; Member Calvin H. Wiley Literary Society,
Senior Scientific Club, Glee Club, Athletic Association.

CELESTE RUDACIL

"Tess"

"Patience and gentleness is power."

Statistician Senior Black and Gold; Secretary World Events Club (second term); Senior Baseball Team; Member Rooters' Club, Hiking Club, La Cercle Francaise, Athletic Association.

ALFRED EUGENE HOLTON

"Gene"

"A town that boasts inhabitants like me, Can have no lack of good society."

Executive Committee Senior Class; Program Committee Senior Class; Associate Business Manager Black and Gold; Statistician Senior Black and Gold; Manager Basketball; Manager Senior Football; Chief Cheer Leader Athletic Association; Member Hi-Y Club, Calvin H. Wiley Literary Society, Societas Litterarum, Athletic Association.

ELIZABETH ETHEL BROOKS

"Et"

"Life was made for noble deeds."

Member Rooters' Club, La Cercle Francaise, Athletic Association.

JOHN NELSON STILL, JR.

"Still"

"Who is it can read a woman?"

Senior Baseball Team; Member Calvin H. Wiley Literary Society, Societas Litterarum, Athletic Association.

ANNA BEATRICE DIXON

"Bea" "Puttin"

"Nothing endures but personal qualities."

Member World Events Club, Rooters' Club, Hiking Club, Athletic Association.

LINDSAY ALVIS LANCASTER

"Lanky"

"You may depend upon it that he is a good man whose intimate friends are all good."

Member Calvin H. Wiley Literary Society, World Events Club, Athletic Association.

LILLIAN RUFFIN CROMER

"Lilly"

*"Cheerful at morn she wakes
from short repose,
Breathes the keen air and
carols as she goes."*

Treasurer Senior Class; Executive Committee; Statistician Senior Black and Gold; Vote Committee Senior Class; Varsity Basketball; Varsity Tennis; Cheer Leader Rooters' Club; President La Cercle Francaise; Chairman Bulletin Board Committee Twentieth Century Thinkers' Club (second term); Member Hiking Club, Athletic Association.

THELMA KATHRYNE RICHARDSON

"Dick"

"No friend was to her unwelcome."

Executive Committee; Statistician Senior Black and Gold; Associate Editor Black and Gold; Senior Baseball Team; Chairman Bulletin Board Committee World Events Club (first term); Chairman Program Committee La Cercle Francaise; Member Hiking Club, Rooters' Club, Athletic Association.

CLARENCE ODELL SAPP

"Spec"

"An artist should have more than two eyes."

Art Editor Black and Gold; Fun-Maker Senior Black and Gold; Varsity Baseball; Sergeant-at-arms Scientific Club; Member Hi-Y Club, Calvin H. Wiley Literary Society, Societas Litterarum, Monogram Club, Glee Club, Athletic Association.

MARGARET FRANCES LENTZ

"Laeke"

"She is good, easier to forgive than to forget."

Varsity Hockey; Varsity Basketball; Senior Baseball Team; Vice-President Rooters' Club; Vice-President World Events Club (first term); Member La Cercle Francaise, Hiking Club, Athletic Association.

EDWIN LINK STOCKTON

"Ed"

"It is in learning music that many youthful hearts learn love."

Captain Senior Baseball Team; Treasurer Hi-Y Club; Member Calvin H. Wiley Literary Society, Societas Litterarum, Scientific Club, Band, Orchestra, Athletic Association.

PEARL KATHLEEN LONGWORTH

"Meggy"

"The bird that flutters least is longest on the wing."

Winner 11th Grade Penmanship Contest; Member World Events Club, Athletic Association.

JAMES DAVID MCSWAIN

"Jim" "Dark Horse"

"Of manners gentle, of affections strong, a man for business all along."

Sergeant-at-arms Senior Class; Fun-Maker Senior Black and Gold; Member Calvin H. Wiley Literary Society, Societas Litterarum, La Cercle Francaise, Athletic Association.

ANNIE MOSELLE STEPHENSON

"Moses"

"What she wills to do or say seems wisest, most virtuous, discreetest, best."

Secretary Senior Class; Executive Committee; Library Page; Varsity Basketball; Varsity Tennis; President Athletic Association; Chairman Bulletin Board Committee Twentieth Century Thinkers' Club (first term); Member Rooters' Club, La Cercle Francaise, Hiking Club.

ROBERT HOYLE STAMPER

"Oil"

"Who thinks all science, as all virtue, vain."

Library Page; Senior Football Team; Senior Basketball Team; Chairman Program Committee Senior Scientific Club; Member Hi-Y Club, Athletic Association.

LENA VIOLA WEST

"Sleepy" "Deeder"

"The sweetest garland to the sweetest maid."

Vice-President Senior Class; Typewriting Team; President World Events Club (first term); Member Rooters' Club, Hiking Club, Athletic Association.

THOMAS BENJAMIN VICK

"Tom"

"It is tranquil people who accomplish much."

Member World Events Club, Spanish Club, Athletic Association.

MARY CAROLINE CROUSE

"Fritz"

"Gentle of speech, beneficent of mind."

Member Rooters' Club, World Events Club, Hiking Club, Athletic Association.

TARASA MARGARET GRAHAM

"Tady"

"Her voice was as sweet and musical as Appolo's lute."

Class Prophet; Assistant Manager Basketball; Member La Cercle Francaise, Twentieth Century Thinkers' Club, Hiking Club, Rooters' Club, Athletic Association.

CHARLES WALTER SNYDER, JR.

"Walt"

"One science only will one genius fit, So vast is art, so narrow human wit."

Senior Baseball Team; Member Calvin H. Wiley Literary Society, Societas Litterarum, Senior Scientific Club, Athletic Association.

WILMA LUCILE PULLIAM

"Billy"

"Genuine and innocent wit is surely the very flavor of the mind."

Vice-President World Events Club (second term); Member Rooters' Club, Hiking Club, Athletic Association.

ALLEN WOOSLEY PEGRAM

"Piggy"

"Neither above nor below his business."

Senior Football Team; Senior Baseball Team; Member Hi-Y Club, Societas Litterarum, Spanish Club, Athletic Association.

INA STAMPER

"Ina"

"Her voice was ever soft, gentle, and low; an excellent thing in woman."

Member La Cercle Francaise, Twentieth Century Thinkers' Club, Rooters' Club, Hiking Club, Athletic Association.

RALPH LEWIS FRAZIER

"Bill"

"Men of few words are the best men."

Varsity Football; Varsity Track; Senior Baseball Team; Secretary and Treasurer Monogram Club; Vice-President Twentieth Century Thinkers' Club; Member Spanish Club, La Cercle Francaise, Scientific Club, Athletic Association.

CORDELIA GRIGG SHANER

"Cotton" "Shanah"

"She has an eye that could speak though her tongue were silent."

Statistician Senior Black and Gold; Fun-Maker Senior Black and Gold; Varsity. Basketball; Varsity Tennis; President Twentieth Century Thinkers' Club; Secretary Rooters' Club; Member La Cercle Francaise, Hiking Club, Athletic Association.

COOPER D. CASS

"Cooper Darling"

"Wit and humor belong to genius alone."

Associate Editor Black and Gold; Chief Fun-Maker Senior Black and Gold; Writer Senior Class Will; Varsity Football; Basketball Squad; Senior Baseball Team; Member Calvin H. Wiley Literary Society, Monogram Club, Societas Litterarum, Athletic Association.

LOUISE ELIZABETH JOHNSTON

"Louise" "Dink"

"Good humor is the clear blue sky of the soul."

Member La Cercle Francaise, Hiking Club, Twentieth Century Thinkers' Club, Rooters' Club, Athletic Association.

NEWTON CROMWELL EBAUGH

"Newt"

"Look, he's winding up the watch of his wit; by and by it will strike."

Business Manager Black and Gold; Statistician Senior Black and Gold; Senior Football Team; Senior Basketball Team; Secretary Hi-Y Club; Member Calvin H. Wiley Literary Society, Societas Litterarum, La Cercle Francaise, Athletic Association.

ELIZABETH MEINUNG

"Dido" "Lib"

"There is no beauty on earth which exceeds the natural loveliness of woman."

Member La Cercle Francaise, Hiking Club, Twentieth Century Thinkers' Club, Rooters' Club, Athletic Association.

HENRY NADING HEITMAN

"Enrique"

"He has something better to do than talk."

Typewriting Team; Treasurer Spanish Club; President World Events Club; Member Calvin H. Wiley Literary Society, Athletic Association.

IVA MAYE TUCKER

"Tucker"

"Charms strike the sight, but merit wins the soul."

Member La Cercle Francaise, Twentieth Century Thinkers' Club, Rooters' Club, Hiking Club, Athletic Association.

MARGARET LALLIS BROOKES

"Peggie"

"A smile for all,
A greeting glad,
A friendly, jolly way she had."

Statistician Senior Black and Gold; Senior Basketball Team; Manager Hiking Club; Member La Cercle Francaise, Twentieth Century Thinkers' Club, Rooters' Club.

HOWARD VANDYKE TRIVETTE

"Chiney"

"Languages are the pedigree of nations."

Member Hi-Y Club, Calvin H. Wiley Literary Society, Societas Litterarum, Spanish Club, Athletic Association.

GRACE ADELINE CAUDLE

"Pete" "Dump"

*"As sweet and musical as
Apollo's lute."*

Statistician Senior Black and Gold;
Senior Baseball Team; Member Root-
ers' Club, Hiking Club, World Events
Club, Athletic Association.

RICHARD CASWELL HORNE

"Rich" "Bull"

"There is no tax on words."

Associate Editor Black and Gold;
President Calvin H. Wiley Literary
Society; Debating Team; Member So-
cietas Litterarum, Glee Club, Athletic
Association.

MILDRED HARRIET RUSS

"Milly" "Butterfly"

*"Far may we search before we find
A heart so gentle and so kind."*

Statistician Senior Black and Gold;
Manager Senior Basketball; Track
Team; Member La Cercle Francaise,
Twentieth Century Thinkers' Club,
Hiking Club, Rooters' Club, Athletic
Association.

LOLA MAYE SIMPSON

"Duck"

*"Her heart was as great as the world,
but there was no room in it to hold the
memory of a wrong."*

Fun-Maker Senior Black and Gold;
Manager Girls' Baseball; Varsity
Basketball; Senior Baseball Team;
Member World Events Club, La Cer-
cle Francaise, Rooters' Club, Hiking
Club, Athletic Association.

MARION BOLICK

"Bo"

*"It is the soul that makes the body
rich."*

Football Squad; Track Team; Senior
Basketball Team; Member Hi-Y Club,
Societas Litterarum, Senior Scientific
Club, Athletic Association.

CRYSTAL MARION STEELMAN

"Krys"

"A tender heart, a will inflexible."

Member La Cercle Francaise, Twentieth Century Thinkers' Club, Rooters'
Club, Athletic Association.

CHARLES EVERETTE HAMILTON, JR.

"Charlie"

"Judge me by my walk, by my talk, or by my countenance; for I am ashamed of none."

Executive Committee; Associate Editor Black and Gold; Program Committee Calvin H. Wiley Literary Society; Debating Team; Senior Baseball Team; Senior Tennis Team; Member Hi-Y Club, Societas Litterarum, Athletic Association.

HELEN ELIZABETH BAGBY

"Bag"

"As merry as the day is long."

Member Rooters' Club, Twentieth Century Thinkers' Club, La Cercle Francaise, Hiking Club, Athletic Association.

HANSELLE LINDSAY HESTER

"Jerry"

"Thou living ray of intellectual fire."

Associate Editor Black and Gold; Library Page; Debating Team; Emory and Henry State-wide Declaiming Contest; President Societas Litterarum (second term); Program Committee Calvin H. Wiley Literary Society; Member Hi-Y Club, Athletic Association.

GRACE WINIFRED HIATT

"Gish" "Gaet"

"The burden becomes lighter which is cheerfully borne."

Member World Events Club, Hiking Club, Rooters' Club, Athletic Association.

GEORGE CLINTON HOLROYD

"Shorty"

"In the scale of destinies, brawn will never weigh so much as brain."

Editor-in-Chief Black and Gold; Secretary Calvin H. Wiley Literary Society; Vice-President and Press Reporter Senior Scientific Club; Member Athletic Association.

ANNIE GRAHAM CALDWELL

"Punch"

"Her unselfishness and kindness have won for her many friends."

Writer Senior Class Will; Member Twentieth Century Thinkers' Club, La Cercle Francaise, Hiking Club, Athletic Association.

SAMUEL HUGHES ADAMS

"Sam"

"In framing an artist, art hath thus decreed
To make some good but others to exceed."

Associate Art Editor Black and Gold; Fun-Maker Senior Black and Gold; Member Calvin H. Wiley Literary Society, Hi-Y Club, Progressive Thinkers' Club, Scientific Club, Athletic Association.

SARAH EDNA BRAY

"Sally"

"A creature not too bright or good
For human nature's daily food."

Member Rooters' Club, La Cercle Francaise, Hiking Club, Athletic Association.

PEYTON BRYANT ABBOTT

"Abbie"

"True as the dial to the sun."

Library Page; Captain Senior Football Team; Chairman Bulletin Board Committee Societas Litterarum (first term); Vice-President Spanish Club; Member Athletic Association.

ROSA TERESA HONEY

"Doda"

*"A merry heart goes all the day,
A sad tires within a mile."*

Member World Events Club, La Cercle Francaise, Rooters' Club, Hiking Club, Athletic Association.

JOHN RUSSELL FULP

"Lefty"

"He locks his knowledge in his head."

Varsity Baseball; Member Twentieth Century Thinkers' Club, Athletic Association.

ELEANOR HOLMES FRANKLIN

"Elna" "Jo"

"Inner sunshine warms not only the heart of the owner, but all who come in contact with it."

Statistician Senior Black and Gold; Library Page; Senior Basketball Team; Manager Senior Hockey; President Twentieth Century Thinkers' Club (first term); Member Rooters' Club, La Cercle Francaise, Hiking Club, Athletic Association.

Oscar Benjamin Eaton, Jr.

"Ben" "Sparky"

"For thoughts are so great, aren't they, Sir,
They seem to lie upon us like a deep flood?"

Associate Editor Black and Gold; Senior Football Team; Senior Tennis Team; Winner Bronze Medal State-wide Declamation Contest at Wake Forest; Chairman Program Committee Calvin H. Wiley Literary Society; Member Hi-Y Club, Societas Litterarum, Glee Club, Athletic Association.

Emma Louise Parrish

"Dimples"

"A gem of purest ray serene."

Statistician Senior Black and Gold; Fun-Maker Senior Black and Gold; Senior Basketball Team; Vice-President Twentieth Century Thinkers' Club (first term); Member La Cercle Francaise, Rooters' Club, Hiking Club, Athletic Association.

Clarence Reginald Graham

"Happy am I; from care I'm free.
Why aren't they all contented like me?"

Chief Statistician Senior Black and Gold; Varsity Swimming; Senior Football Team; Senior Basketball Team; Member Hi-Y Club, Societas Litterarum, Glee Club, Senior Scientific Club, Athletic Association.

EVA GERTRUDE EARLY

"Adam" "Eva"

"Modesty is to merit what shade is to figures in a picture; it gives it strength and makes it stand out."

Member World Events Club, Hiking Club, Athletic Association.

SAMUEL HARRIS CHAMBERLAIN

"Monk"

"True to his word, work, and his friends."

Associate Business Manager Black and Gold; Senior Football Team; Senior Baseball Team; Member Calvin H. Wiley Literary Society, Senior Scientific Club, Societas Litterarum, Athletic Association.

MARY ELIZABETH CONRAD

"Lib"

"She maketh her path light with good humor."

Writer Senior Class Will; Senior Baseball Team; Member Rooters' Club, World Events Club, Hiking Club, Athletic Association.

SAMUEL FRANCIS DAVIS

"Boll Weevil"

"To live as gently as I can; to be, no matter where, a man"

Varsity Football; Senior Baseball Team; Member Monogram Club, Hi-Y Club, Glee Club, Calvin H. Wiley Literary Society, Athletic Association.

DORIS MARY COX

"Dot"

"Our thoughts and our conduct are our own."

Typewriting Team; Member Rooters' Club, World Events Club, Hiking Club, Athletic Association.

HAZEL THELMA CONRAD

"Bug" "Hadie"

"Her modest looks the cottage might adorn,
Sweet as the primrose peeps beneath the thorn."

Member Rooters' Club, Hiking Club, La Cercle Francaise, World Events Club, Athletic Association.

OWEN ALEXANDER. CHATHAM

"Swan" "Chat"

"They are only truly great who are truly good."

Executive Committee; Class Historian; Fun-Maker Senior Black and Gold; Associate Editor Black and Gold; Varsity Football; President Senior Hi-Y Club; Vice-President Societas Litterarum; Member Monogram Club, Calvin H. Wiley Literary Society, Glee Club, Athletic Association.

MARY LOUISE DALTON

"Sister"

"As pure as a pearl, and as perfect: A noble and innocent girl."

Library Page; Secretary Twentieth Century Thinkers' Club (first term); Member La Cercle Francaise, Hiking Club, Rooters' Club, Athletic Association.

FRANCIS DE VANE JENKINS

"Frank"

"That all softening, overpowering knell.
The tocsin of the soul, the dinner bell."

Senior Football Team; Senior Basketball Team; Member Hi-Y Club, Societas Litterarum, Athletic Association.

ISABELLE BOST

"Izzy"

"Beholding the bright countenance of truth in the quiet and still air of delightful studies."

Member Twentieth Century Thinkers' Club, La Cercle Francaise, Rooters' Club, Hiking Club, Athletic Association.

WALTER FRANCIS NEWMAN

"Walt"

"All things come round to him who will but wait."

Football Squad; Track Squad; Member Calvin H. Wiley Literary Society, Societas Litterarum, La Cercle Francaise, Athletic Association.

MABEL JOSEPHINE TRIVETTE

"Billy" "Polly"

"A good heart's worth gold."

Member La Cercle Francaise, Twentieth Century Thinkers' Club, Rooters' Club, Hiking Club, Athletic Association.

HAZEL MARIE KEARNS

"Hazel"

"The thing that goes farthest towards making life worth while, that costs the least, and does the most, is just a pleasant smile."

Varsity Basketball; Member La Cercle Francaise, Rooters' Club, Hiking Club, Athletic Association.

RICHARD BEVERLY HARWOOD

"Rich"

"I love tranquil solitude and such society as is quiet, wise, and good."

Member Hi-Y Club, World Events Club, Athletic Association.

MARY JOSEPHINE HUNTLEY

"Jo"

"A face with gladness overspread; Soft smiles, by human kindness bred."

Varsity Basketball; Tennis Champion; Secretary Twentieth Century Thinkers' Club; Member La Cercle Francaise, Hiking Club, Athletic Association.

PAULINE FIELD GRIFFITH

"Polly"

"Books are the ever burning lamps of accumulated wisdom."

Member Twentieth Century Thinkers' Club, La Cercle Francaise, Rooters' Club, Athletic Association.

JOHN SHAW FOSTER, JR.

"Johnny"

"Content to do the best work he could, to preserve his own dignity, to leave the rest to the future."

Associate Editor Black and Gold; Chairman Vote Committee; Press Reporter Calvin H. Wiley Literary Society; Varsity Tennis Basketball squad Cheer Leader Athletic Association; Vice-President Senior Hi-Y Club; President Societas Litterarum; Member Monogram Club, Glee Club, Athletic Association.

The Journey

(Class Poem)

I

Four years ago we started out—
 A jolly, happy crew,
Upon the Sea of Knowledge, and we've
 Sailed the briny blue
Until today. But now we're set
 For a journey full of strife;
We've raised our mast and trimmed our sails,
 "Ahoy! the Sea of Life!"

II

But, what! This jolly, happy crew,
 Are we ready to set sail?
Do we know the many danger points
 This journey will entail?
There are rocks of grave disaster;
 Selfishness and jagged Pride;
Sea Monsters, ugly Greed and Hate,
 Leer in the foaming tide.

III

But yes! this jolly, happy crew
 Can steer without a wreck;
We've been banded close together,
 Ever watchful, on the deck.
We have had the bravest captains,
 Helpful, kind, and quick to praise,
Guiding, keeping little sailors
 In the water's smoothest ways.

IV

Now we're starting on the journey,
 With our motto waving high
O'er the seething rolling waters,
 Pointing upward to the sky.
We will hope to reach the harbor,
 Whether north, or south or west;
But we're sailing for a shining goal,
 Each one bound to do his best.
                    —*Dore Davis* '24·

Class History

OUR CLASS started into high school, as classes usually do as freshmen. We were pretty fresh, too; and those were the good old days when freshmen (boys) were subject to the paddle of the upper classmen. We got our share. We went thru a year of freshie-dom which, although routine in so far as freshmen in general are concerned, was all important to us because we were all-important to ourselves. Were we not high school students? Pupils, at any rate. When we would go back to the old schools from whence we came, we would be pointed out as "one of them high school fellers."

We came in for our full show of honors and distinctions, too, several of our number having won prizes on Thrift Essays, and one, our present president, Miss Evelyn Morris, having won the coveted first Kiwanis Cup; our pride and self-importance were not diminished by these little recognitions of our worth. We finished our first year of "high" life with a feeling that we had already started on the road to fame and fortune.

Well, about two-thirds of our number came back next year, and we were "sophomores", which means, literally, wise fools. This time we came feeling a little less important to ourselves, perhaps, and possibly we were a little more important to the classes ahead of us; and I know we were of importance to the class below us—that is, until a rule was passed prohibiting the use of boards and other utensils on the anatomy of male freshmen. Nothing of great importance happened that year; we were young yet, and all we were supposed to do was to study hard—which some of us did—and to be careful not to abuse the one senior privilege of using the front door (there are no such privileges now). We simply cast one more grindstone behind us in the form of a grade.

The junior class was a family of a little less than half of the number we had been as freshmen; I say family because we had all of the traits of a real family, brothers, sisters, quarrels, fusses, cats, etc. It was in that year that things really began to happen. That was our first introduction to politics, and when we think of what has come about since, politically speaking, we are glad that that introduction was mild in form. We organized the class and elected as president the right Honorable John Shaw Foster, Jr., whose staff was composed of the following notables: O. Ben Eaton, Jr., vice-president; Miss Evelyn Morris, secretary; and Miss Laeke Lentz, treasurer. This was a very efficient staff, with about five exceptions.

That year we followed the well defined custom of entertaining the seniors at the Hallowe'en time. It was a gala affair. The old High School had its timbers shivered by the sound of rollicking laughter and song, while the faces of both boys and girls shown with happiness, (the girls having forgotten their do-rains, or whatever you call these little tin boxes with a mirror and a sponge in one side and a cake of Bon Ami in the other, which they use). This reception was enjoyed by the seniors, so they said, and those of the juniors who had not been placed on committees; and even those who served on committees enjoyed the trip home, "after the ball was over" (?).

A few weeks later there came a red-letter day in the lives of all of us; it was not the end of a report period, either. The day dawned bright and early, as the days have a habit of doing, and we all came to school more or less on time. That day at chapel period they explained to us a brand new set of rules; we were told just how each student was to leave the building in case of fire. Accepting them as just "some more laws," we thought nothing of it at the time; but that night—joy of joys, sorrow of sorrows, suspicion of suspicions, horror of horrors—the old High School burned! ! 1 1 The thing which every school-boy and girl has fondly dreamed of had happened to us; a holiday was almost inevitable, but our long cherished dream was short-lived. The glorious tragedy came on Wednesday. On Monday next, we entered the magnificent new structure which was being erected for our special benefit, the R. J. R. M. H. S. of W.-S., N. C. Finishing the year out here in the country, we were taught readin', 'ritin', 'rithmetic, and rules (Mr. Koos having been installed in the faculty), to the tune of the song of the birds, the slam-bang hammering of the carpenters, the music of the riveting machines, and the incessant but melodious lowing and cackling of Mr. Haltiwanger's kine and poultry.

At the end of that eventful year, several of us became seniors, in name, and, of course, in work, but not in mind; few of us have yet come to a full realization of the fact that we are really and truly, honest-to-grandmother seniors.

When we became seniors, we had another dose of politics; a new kind of politics—woman suffrage, in which the boys did the suffering, and frame-up politics, in which the boys tried to frame, but got framed —and, consequently, "frammed." The result of the class election was, femininely speaking, as follows: Miss Evelyn Morris, president; Miss Lena West, vice-president; Miss Moselle Stephenson, secretary; Miss Lillian Cromer, treasurer; and Miss Hazel Hauser, reporter. Masculinely speaking, the result was: an awfully, woefully, horribly, humorously uncomfortable state of affairs. Well, we went ahead with our feminine regal troupe, until after a while the said royalty decided that possibly some of the boys might, by some freak of nature, "have a few ideas that the girls would sanction and agree to"; so they roped a few boys and some more girls—boys in minority—into what was called an Executive Committee, which in reality was a clever scheme for gyping the boys into thinking that they had some part in the administration of the class.

As every history must have its tragedy, so our darkest hour came when we lost our true friend and schoolmate, Leo Caldwell, who gave his life striving for the honor and ideals of our school. We mourn our great loss, and pause in loving tribute to his memory.

We went on thru the year, having our big-time, bang-up class meetings, until finally the question arose as to whether the juniors thought we expected them to give us a reception or not, they having already given their reception money for a better cause. It was decided that, to eliminate embarrassment and to have a good time, we should have a "two-bit" party, and dispense with the customary Junior-Senior Reception for this year. When the gates were opened, at about eight bells, the juniors and seniors began to show up, and we were still here when the man called "bed-time". On this occasion the presidents of the two classes, one being a boy and the other a girl, thereby making them eligible, were joined in (mock) matrimony, thus joining the two classes in (apparent) friendship. During the course of the evening, all of us were happy some of the time; for instance, when the eats were served—or rather, put where we could get at them. Some of us were happy all of the time; an example, "Fat" Hendrix and Sara Bray. But all of us were not happy all of the time; it was a leap-year party. The suffragettes exercised their leap-year privileges so far as asking for dates was concerned, but when it came to shelling out for the street-car fares, and seeing the boys safely home, they were decidedly feminine.

Among the most interesting of our pastimes during our sojourn in the senior class has been the enjoyment we have gotten from watching the numerous and divers infatuations and love affairs, which have by no means been confined to our classmates; certain members of the faculty have contributed their full share, and have thereby come in for their full share of teasing, etc.

We are finishing out the year in fine style; some of us are passing our work, too, and we are looking forward to the time when we will sit on the mantel-piece of the new R. J. R. Auditorium, and receive the long cherished sheepskins for which we have so earnestly and conscientiously striven.

—*Hazel Hauser*
—*Owen Chatham*

Last Will and Testament

State of North Carolina, ⎫
County of Forsyth, ⎬ RICHARD J. REYNOLDS HIGH SCHOOL.
City of Winston-Salem. ⎭

E, THE Senior Class of 1924, of the Richard J. Reynolds High School of Winston-Salem, North Carolina, being about to pass out of this sphere of education, realizing the frailties and uncertainties of human existence, and being in full possession of a crammed mind and almost superhuman understanding, do make and publish this our Last Will and Testament, hereby revoking and declaring void all wills by us at any time heretofore made. As to the estates which the Fates and High Cost of Living have allowed us to accumulate we make the following disposition, viz.:

FIRST: To our beloved Superintendent, Mr. R. H. Latham, we, the Seniors of '24, do bequeath our sincere affections, our deepest reverence, our deepest gratitude, and the unlimited wealth of our memory forever.

SECOND: To Mr. Moore we will the stepping stones to achievement, over which he has helped us so gloriously, that he may hold them as an example to the incoming Senior Class.

THIRD: To the dear faculty, who have been our instructors in all the wisdom of the ages, we leave a sweet and unbroken succession of restful nights and peaceful dreams. They have all done their duty and verily now shall they have their well earned reward.

FOURTH: To our Marshalls we leave our sincerest regards for the many deeds of kindness they have shown us.

FIFTH: To the incoming Senior Class we will our dignity, together with our privileges and positions. May they uphold them forever, with all seriousness and gravity, endeavoring to realize their vast importance.

SIXTH: To the classes of '25, '26, and '27 we leave our blessings, tender memories of our pleasant associations together, our forgiveness for anything that we may not have exactly appreciated in the demonstrations of the past, and a pledge of friendship forever.

SEVENTH: To the incoming Freshmen Class we will all chewing gum that may be found under typewriters, chairs, desks, tables, and in locker rooms; with this note to them that they always find a safe and secure place to conceal it before going to class, or before making a visit to the office.

EIGHTH: To Archie Shreves we leave Owen Chatham's height. We hope he will use it in such an elevating way, that he will always find himself above his classmates.

NINTH: We gladly will "Pet" Sheppard's athletic ability to Frances Hahn, and may she guard and protect it with great success.

TENTH: To Frances Chandler we leave Mae Simpson's sportsmanship. May she use it as Mae has, and may she ever hold it as an example to her fellow classmates.

ELEVENTH: We lovingly will to Homer Houchins the numerous love affairs with prominent seniors (especially T. G.) of Paul Murphy; and we hope he will rush them forward with the same zeal and persistence that Paul has shown.

TWELFTH: We do solemnly will Laeke Lentz's athletic ability to the Freshman who failed to make the basketball team last year.

THIRTEENTH: To Joe Petree we leave Russell Fulp's ability to sleep during class and get away with it. May the class of next year provide him with a pillow, that his dreams may be more peaceful.

FOURTEENTH: To Eva Lee Kinnely we do hereby will Tarasa Graham's art of talking, and hope that she may use it to the good advantage that Tarasa has.

FIFTEENTH: To Elizabeth Atkins we leave Mildred Russ's ability to giggle.

SIXTEENTH: To "Blitz" Dillard we leave Eleanor Franklin's habit of rolling her eyes, and hope that it will be the service to her it has been to Eleanor.

SEVENTEENTH: To Henry Roan we bequeath Jim McSwain's "windbroken" pony in which is pure Latin blood, and we pray that he will give it at least one day of rest during next school term, for it certainly has not received any heretofore.

EIGHTEENTH: Knowing that our class is overloaded with vocal talent, we very gratefully bequeath Hoyle Stamper's fine voice to Bud Harper, who we hope will use it in a quieter way than Hoyle has.

NINETEENTH: To Ella Cannon Hill, we leave the flapper ways of Margaret Brooks. Our wish is that she may become as efficient as Margaret.

TWENTIETH: We leave Pauline Griffith's wonderful gift of arguing to Elizabeth Gentry, and we sincerely hope that she may use it successfully.

TWENTY-FIRST: To Robert L. Hatcher we leave Hanselle Hester's ability to talk on any subject, at any place, and at any time, and also for any length of time.

TWENTY-SECOND: To "Cake" Parnell we leave Richard Horne's ability as a "cake-eater" and to carry crumbs in his pockets, realizing he is a willing understudy and follows daily in "Poor Richard's" footsteps.

TWENTY-THIRD: To Caroline Price we leave Evelyn Morris's art as a musician, and hope that it will lift her to the social position Evelyn has attained.

TWENTY-FOURTH: We leave Helen Bagby's advoirdupois to Virginia Dunklee.

TWENTY-FIFTH: To Russell Plaster we leave Frank Davis's good looks, and "sheiky" ways.

TWENTY-SIXTH: We leave a little of Bill Frazier's common sense to Tom Clingman, realizing the dire need on the one hand and the superfluity on the other.

TWENTY-SEVENTH: To Clayton McMichael we leave Nelson Still's laziness and ability to stay in High School eight years, including four summer schools.

TWENTY-EIGHTH: We leave Louise Dalton's quality of not talking to Joyce Warner.

TWENTY-NINTH: To Lois Strickland we leave Tarasa Graham's immense height.

THIRTIETH: To "Egg" Ford we leave Curtis Lane's vanity case, consisting of comb, brush, and all necessary cosmetics that are required in the present-day make-up.

Lastly, we, as a parting gift, leave to the High School Oscar Q. Crotts and his lovely red locks, realizing that it is a lingering donation, and will occupy space for years to come.

And we do hereby appoint and constitute J. M. Shields sole executor of this our Last Will and Testament.

In witness whereof, we, the Class of '24, the testators, have to this, our will, set our hands and seal, this, the fifth day of June, Anno Domini one thousand nine hundred and twenty-four.

Witnesses: Seal:
   MR. E. K. McNEW,   COOPER D. CASS,
   MISS MARY C. WILEY,   ANNIE GRAHAM CALDWELL,
   MISS ANNA LULA DOBSON.   ELIZABETH CONRAD.

Most Popular
Lillian Cromer
Owen Chatham

Best All-round
John Foster
Moselle Stephenson

Best Looking
Celeste Rudacil
Owen Chatham

Best Athletes
"Pet" Sheppard
"Bill" Frazier

Best Sports
Maye Simpson
John Foster

Biggest Flirts
"Bill" Frazier
Cordelia Shaner

Distinctions

GIRLS		BOYS
Lillian Cromer	—Most Popular—	Owen Chatham
Moselle Stephenson	—Best All-round—	John Foster
Celeste Rudacil	—Best Looking—	Owen Chatham
"Pet" Sheppard	—Best Athletes—	"Bill" Frazier
Maye Simpson	—Best Sports—	John Foster
Cordelia Shaner	—Biggest Flirts—	"Bill" Frazier
Elizabeth Meinung	—Laziest—	Nelson Still
Eleanor Franklin	—Jolliest—	Cooper Cass
Eleanor Franklin	—Biggest Eaters—	"Bill" Frazier
Mary Crouse	—Biggest Feet—	Frank Davis
Tarasa Graham	—Most Loquacious—	Richard Horne
Tarasa Graham	—Wittiest—	Eugene Holton
Mildred Russ	—Biggest Giggler—	Paul Murphy
Margaret Brookes	—Cutest—	Russell Fulp
Margaret Brookes	—Biggest Flapper—Cake-Eater—	Richard Horne
Lillian Cromer	—Peppiest—	Eugene Holton

Super Distinctions

"Pet" Sheppard	—Most Dignified—	Eugene Holton
Ethel Brookes	—Most Studious—	Nelson Still
"Jo" Huntley	—Fattest—	Curtis Lane

Class Prophecy

SCENE: Dimly lighted room. In the only spot of light Mr. McNew is sitting in a comfortable chair leaning back "listening in" on this:

This is K. D. K. A., East Pittsburgh, Penn. We have with us this evening Mr. Richard Horne who is to speak to us on "Our Class of '24 and What We Have Done in Ten Years."

Mr. Horne:

"Ladies and what you have with you, I am here this evening to endeavor to tell you of our brilliant class and of our success in life. First, you all know (or do you?) that K. D. K. A. belongs to Mr. Francis Jenkins and every one "listening in" knows that this is the pioneer station of the world, the largest and best. (Mr. McNew: "All I know is that you get K. D. K. A. before you even tune in.") One reason for this is that the celebrated Newton Ebaugh sells his inventions to K. D. K. A. Mr. Ebaugh made his 'talked of million' in this way and is now building a mansion for his wife, once his schoolmate now his lifemate. She was Miss-whiz-y-st-a-c-buzz-e-e-k-***!!?? (Mr. Mc-

New: "By Pluto! I don't suppose I'll ever know who she was now.")
er-er-buzz-rr-Sam Adams, Architect.

"We will now be favored with a selection by Miss Jenny
Lasley, who, by the way, is directing all the minstrels in Winston-
Salem now. Miss Lasley: (Soft music with a crashing chord wind-
ing through.)

(Mr. McNew: "Oh! music hath charms to soothe the savage
beasts—maybe that's why some folks enjoy it so much.")

"We have just received a telegram from Dr. Isabell Bost, Chi-
cago, Ill., saying: 'Program coming in fine. Must say I'm enjoy-
ing it.'

"Peyton Abbott is Winston-Salem's leading lawyer; he has just
won for Allen Pegram his divorce from N—stac—whizzz!) * * * *

(Mr. McNew: "Um-m—Yes, Mars, that's another good man
gone crazy.") "Miss Adela Sheppard has discovered the real fountain of youth and is growing younger each day. This wonderful
fountain is located in—qui—eee—et—whee—x—. (Mr. McNew:
"Oh, Venus, have pity. Now, of all times, especially now! Just when
I'm beginning to need it, too!")

"Crystal Steelman and Helen Bagby are our two best bets as the
real movie stars of '34·

"Jim Shore is teaching in the public schools of Richmond, Va.

"Tarasa Graham is the companion of Mrs. Prince of Wales,
nee Annie Graham Caldwell, who is traveling in India with Mr.
Prince, who isn't king yet.

"We all knew that Ralph Choplin was ambitious to be a lawyer,
but as there was too much competition in that field he has kindly
consented to be our next governor.

"A new music store has opened up on Liberty Street in Winston-
Salem featuring this sign: Grow Tall to Music. Stockton & Lane.
Stockton Makes the Music, Lane the Noise to Accompany It.

"Robert Foltz has given up music as a profession and is now
a soda jerker at Woolworths 5c and 10c Store.

"Grace Hiatt has become one of the greatest authorities on
history in the city. We all knew Grace was good on history but
had never predicted such a wonderful career for her.

"Maye Simpson and Laeke Lentz are about to put the firm of
Bocock and Stroud out of business. Being athletes of the first order,
they naturally turned to this kind of business and are able to give
first-hand information with each sale of athletic goods.

"Josephine Huntley and Odell Sapp have painted the masterpiece
of the year. Their gifted brush and faithful memory have painted
the beautiful High School and Auditorium—the fence enclosing it

is indeed a wonderful piece of workmanship. This painting hangs in Le Louvre. .

"Madame Fanchette (an old friend, Hazel Hauser) is making piles of money with her unique designs of clothing. .They rank with Platon et Lucille.

"Hoyle Stamper is now with Ziegfield. He gained his position by being able to solve all problems dealing with figures.

(Mr. McNew: "Now, that wouldn't suit some aesthetic tastes.")

"Mary Ackerman, after ten years of hunting a husband, has married a teacher of the Hanestown High School. They have started a school teaching old maids the art of Love-making. Beatrice Dixon and Hazel Conrad are their most promising pupils.

"John S. Foster, Jr., is now the United States Tennis Champion. He plays the Austrian Champion tomorrow.

(Mr. McNew: "Here's luck to you, Johnny, old boy.") .

"You all, no doubt, remember the wonderful work of Moselle Stephenson on the W. H. S. Basketball Team. Well, she is still at it. She is now President of the National Athletic Board.

"Walter Snyder, when not hanging around Kress's, spends his time repairing hearts for ladies only.

"Oscar Crotts, Master of Dancing at Hicksville, announces that he will teach you the holds, and then if you wish to progress farther he will also teach you the steps.

"Ethel Brooks and Rosa Honey have opened the firm of Honey and Brooks. They sell pen points and pencils. These young ladies expect to open up a store in Walkertown soon; that is, in the next twenty years.

"Now Eleanor and Archie Spaugh will render their original song, 'No One Loves As We Do'. These two young people are co-starring in their new venture, 'The Marriage.' (Mr. McNew: "Hum! Ought to be interesting. We must watch these two youngsters. Eh! By the way, I didn't think—fact is, I know Archie belongs to the next class; but they just couldn't separate them, I suppose.")

"Thelma Richardson's ambition is to follow in the footsteps of Mrs. Lindsay Patterson and Lady Astor. We wish her success.

"It will be quite a shock to every one to hear that good little Maye Tucker is in a convent. (Mr. McNew: "We must admit that is a better place than—well! some other places.")

"Elizabeth Meinung is now *Married*—um—such luck—to a doctor who has founded a hospital for invalids.

"Rowena is living up to her name. She has a 'New-Man' nearly every year. She has been married seven times in ten years.

"Lindsay Lancaster, after ten years of work as an assistant mail carrier, has received his promotion and now has a route all by himself.

We are sure that Mr. Lancaster's friends will be glad to hear of his wonderful good fortune.

"Here's a new book just off the press, 'Simplifying and Pronouncing Proper Names', by Rudacil and McClenahan. A good combination, I should think.

"Mr. Russell Fulp, southpaw pitcher for the Yankees, while in Winston-Salem on his vacation, completely demolished his Rolls-Royce by running into a street car. Tom Vick, motorman, says he was 'irresponsible' for the accident.

"Out of the commercial section of W. H. S. we have only a few who really made use of their stenographic course; among these are Wilma Pulliam, Elizabeth Conrad, Mary Crouse, and Doris Cox. All of these *young* ladies are now holding responsible positions in and around this City.

"Frank Bo Davis is Mr. Mathews' assistant since Mr. Shields has a different picture of each student in every issue of the Black and Gold.

"Pauline Griffith is now Dean of an English College For Girls *Only*. (Mr. McNew: "Well, by Cataline, she did do it; but I'll bet she still doesn't know what *inundate* means.")

"Mr. Robert Barton has recently purchased a drug store on South Main Street, near Salem College. Special rates to all Salem vamps, announces Mr. Barton. Mr. Barton is also director of the Moravian Band and is performing a great service to his community by teaching boys and girls in the art of music.

"A telegram has been received just now announcing: 'Tonight at Madison Square Garden a Lecture on Law and It's Effect on the Individual by the Right Honorable Owen Alexander Chatham, former Representative from North Carolina, now considered one of the foremost lawyers and lecturers in this country.'

"Johnston—er—Louise, is now a member of the Chamber of Commerce.

"Evelyn Davis is in the circus. She is the only girl in captivity with long curls. Here's hoping she never cuts them off.

"Henry Heitman won the World's Championship Typewriting Contest with Lena West a close second. Both are now employed as demonstrators by the Underwood Typewriting Company.

"Mabel Trivette is the only missionary our old class can boast of. She is in Korea doing a wonderful work.

"Paul Murphy bought the American Translation Company. The children of W. H. S. daily bless him, especially the seniors, because annually he presents a beautifully bound 'Jack' to every member in the school.

"Hazel Kearns is coach of the basketball team of Winston-Salem

High School. She and Miss Smith have a dandy team there this year. (Mr. McNew: "Yes, Miss Smith, Miss Mary, Miss Dobson, Mr. Moore and I are all that are left of that wonderful faculty which pulled that class of '24 through. We surely had to shut our eyes and push some of them. Them was the happy days!")

"Bill has finally persuaded Gwen that she has waited Long enough for a Count so she has consented to become Mrs. Frazier instead. Bill is coach of football at W. H. S. this year. They won the championship last year and are in a fair line for it this year.

"Contrary to all expectations Richard Harwood has given up his position of Professor of Elocution at Carolina and has bought an interest in the firm of Berger & Hege, retail grocers. Mr. Harwood will make a wonderful addition to the firm.

"Of course we all expected Dore Davis to be a poetess but—whee —sip—bang—(Mr. McNew: "O Jupiter, Pluto, Neptune, Vesta, omnes dies—why, oh, why is it that just when I get interested that blame thing turns off?")—The Davis Baking Powder Company gave her $100.00 for her last one.

"We all knew that Charles was going to make a great success as a lawyer so this announcement will not surprise us: 'Mr. Charles Hamilton was elected Prosecuting Attorney for the State of New York yesterday. He is not yet satisfied and says that he will be Attorney General of the United States of America before his ambition is realized'.

"Peg Brooks is playing that old-fashioned girl of ten years ago, 'The Flapper', in George Holroyd's new play, 'In Ancient Days.' These two young people are counted among the most talented in the country.

"Hanselle Hester and Ben Eaton are having a time. One is Speaker of the House and the other party whip of the Senate. They are of different parties also. There is evidently a hot time in old Washington when both get together.

"Mildred Russ is still studying in Paris. It is rumored that her music master is a prince in disguise and is falling in love with her by inches.

"Daniel Luckenbach succeeded his father as pastor of the Fairview Moravian Church. What a surprise this will be to his classmates, because Daniel did not seem to be a bit ministerially inclined during his high school days.

"Jim McSwaim is the best comedian on the screen. He is also the most beloved movie star and to top it all off is getting the highest wages ever paid a star. On the side he writes humorous stories for the Yadkin Ripple of Yadkinville, N. C.

"Pearl Longworth has gained recognition as one of the best

penmen in the South. This was caused by successful application of the Palmer Method Writing in her high school days.

"Louise Dalton, prima dona—the Bernhardt of America—will be heard in the role of 'Zoza' tonight at the Metropolitan Opera House. Seats selling as high as $350.00.

"Cordelia and Cotton Veach are both coaching football at Elon this year. They couldn't bear to be separated, so Mrs. Veach finally persuaded the faculty of Elon that girls needed football as much as boys.

"Grace Caudle, expert typist and tennis player, will arrive at Washington, July 4, to give a private demonstration before President William Jennings Bryan.

"Lillian Cromer is getting a fabulous salary composing yells and songs for all the schools of America. It seems like old times to go into her studio and hear her practice them. And, by the way, she isn't Miss Cromer anymore—

"A few days ago a member of the class of '24 visited Efird Brothers and was somewhat surprised to see Howard Trivette still holding down his same old job in the shoe department.

"Cooper D. Cass is the biggest box-office attraction in the movies. All the girls are crazy about him, especially Annie Peddycord, who is writing his scenarios.

"Gene Holton won the World's Championship for racing. Gene gave up law for the race track because everyone told him that he was a fast man.

"Emma Parrish is the most popular member of the Columbia University faculty; that is, she teaches between 'good times'. (Mr. McNew: "My word! I wonder how that girl ever heard all that the girls told her when she was called on.")

"Clarence Graham seems to have gone back to his childhood loves. He has the best kennels in the South. His dogs are making him immensely wealthy.

"Walter Newman and Marion Bolick are still freshmen at Carolina. They swore when they went to college that they would make the freshmen football team before they left that class. As I said, they are still freshmen.

"Sam Harris Chamberlain is the best dentist in W. S. Why, even Mr. Koos goes to him.

"Here is a conversation I heard the other day:

First lady: They have wonderful bargains over at the A. & P. Store.

Second lady: Yes, and the manager is so adorable—and fast.

"I looked into the matter and found that it was no one but my old friend Guy Fulp, who was manager of the store.

"There is one member of the class of '24 that is being con-stantly torn between two factions, which are Laziness and Love For the Ladies. All of you can easily guess that it is Nelson Still, and the outcome is very doubtful. He will no doubt make a success at either one.

"Sarah Bray has just completed her latest book, 'A Complete History of the World.' This is in 107 volumes. (Isn't it a shame that Miss Mebane is not at High School to direct the students to use these books as the best references?)

"Eva Early is now running Winston-Salem's Best Beauty Parlor.

"Ina Stamper has founded a remarkable Home For Harmless, Homeless Old Maids. Ina and her husband Mr._____ecke—are the superintendent and assistant superintendent, respectively.

"We will now be favored with a selection by Miss Evelyn Morris—which she aint—she's a Mrs._____. It will be one of her own pieces called 'Senior Politiques'."

(10 minutes later)

This is K. D. K. A. signing off at 12:02 correct time. Good night.

Mr. McNew (stretching and yawning): "Oh Tempora! I didn't realize that it was that late. I must get that jack and run over tomorrow's lesson yet." Goes to door and turns off light.

—*Tarasa M. Graham*
—*Ralph Irvin Choplin*

The Black and Gold

-·Published by the Upper Classes of the Richard J. Reynolds
High School, Winston-Salem, N. C.

Subscription Price - - - - - - - - - One Dollar the Year

EDITORIAL STAFF

GEORGE HOLROYD, '24_____Editor-in-Chief
DORE DAVIS, '24_____Associate Editor-in-Chief

ASSOCIATE EDITORS

HANSELLE HESTER, '24	COOPER D. CASS, '24
RICHARD HORNE, '24	THELMA RICHARDSON, '24
BEN EATON, '24	JOHN FOSTER, '24
OWEN CHATHAM, '24	CHARLES HAMILTON, '24
ROBERT FOLTZ, '24	MAMIE HEGWOOD, '25
PAULINE LINEBERRY, '25	STEPHEN MORRISETT, '25
HAROLD ELLISON, '25	ELIZABETH WILKINSON, '25
MARGARET SPAINHOUR, '26	LORRETTA CARROLL, '26

ODELL SAPP, '24_____Art Editor
SAM ADAMS, '24_____Associate Art Editor
J. PIERSON RICKS, '26_____Associate Art Editor

NEWTON EBAUGH, '24_____Business Manager

ASSOCIATE BUSINESS MANAGERS

EUGENE HOLTON, '24	HARRIS CHAMBERLAIN, '24
EDWARD MICKEY, '25	JOE CARLTON, '25

Faculty Advisor
JAMES M. SHIELDS

For Advertising Rates, Address the Manager

Editorials

INTENTIONS

Are you an intender? Do you belong to that vast organization that always intends but never acts?

We Americans are very generous, very easily affected. We see the other fellow's misfortune and intend to help him. We usually do. The fact is the American people are quicker to see foreign difficulties and flaws than they are to grasp conditions at home. Blubberingly ten millions of dollars are appropriated by Congress to feed the starving children in Germany, while in many American cities and on many farms poverty, suffering and hardships are unalleviated by American contribution. An American soldier, a veteran of the World War, lies dying in a little Virginia town. He has expended the best that is in him for his country's sake. He was greeted by cheering throngs when health and vigor surged through his frame, and when he marched for Uncle Sam. But now, his duty performed, he, neglected and forgotten, is breathing his last of the air that he fought to keep free, while American philanthropists are scraping up additional foreign difficulties to which they might contribute.

Let us use another example. America continues her policy of imperialism, bordering on dictatorship, over the Central and South American countries. She sends American marines to Honduras, let us say, to insure peaceful voting and to guard against the rising up of revolution, "which will affect American commerce." At the same time the American idea of peaceful voting is carried out in the state of Illinois, with the result that only two are killed and several wounded. The moral of this may be construed as: "See that your own dog is quiet, before kicking the other fellow's poodle for howling."

Perhaps these examples have seemed a little far from the topic, so let us come down to the every-day man. Day after day we come in contact with the man who sees the beggar and intends to help him; who hears the cry of the poor and needy and intends to respond; who hears the minister's sermon and intends to consider his salvation; who, perhaps, thinks of his mother's birthday and intends to send her a token of his devotion. What do these intentions amount to? Usually such intentions are merely volatile, they are thought of and then forgotten.

The high school student realizes the opportunity offered him and intends to take full advantage of it. He notes his shortcomings and long-goings and intends to improve. He sees a duty needed to be performed and intends to do it. He sees and intends; he hears and intends; but many times intending is all he does. Intentions without the determination to carry them through are absolutely worthless.

Perhaps, though, after one has failed, after he has ruined himself or his family, it is some consolation to hear: "He intended well." But, regardless of sentiment, the cold, hard fact stares us in the face: the road to hell is paved with good intentions. Does one ever intend to go there? No, he intended to reform, but it was too late.

We citizens of a Christian Community, as students of the Winston-Salem High School, let us learn to carry our "good intentions" through, or else, some day, we, too, may realize that it is too late and that well meant intentions without concentrated actions have been the cause of our ruin.

—H. E.

THAT OLD SPIRIT

As our own Mr. McNew well phrases it, "There is nothing so new as antiquity." Truly, when every heart is anxiously turned to Commencement, when it is the ending of high school days or when the much desired vacation begins, it seems a very inopportune time to stress "school spirit". There is possibly no other one subject that so fills the editorial pages of a school magazine. Yet, just as Mr. McNew says, this ever old subject, if presented right, is ever new and alive.

What is school spirit and what constitutes it? Is it the blind loyalty to our school in the crises, the mere attending of athletic games and the doing of your part in your school's activities, so that your name will go down in the local hall of fame? If this is school spirit —and all that constitutes school spirit— all the school spirit is not worth the ink it takes to print this article, far from justifying this space. Do wild yells and animated spirit when the grid-iron hero dashes sixty yards for an end-run touch-down demonstrate the true essential of school spirit? Does the faithful work of the home-run king when he ends a nine-inning tie, which moves all spectators, re-echo the spirit of a school to a visitor? No, as good and as essential as these are, it does not take school spirit to gain these. Any real red-blooded American's blood blushes in his veins when these take place.

But there is a traditional spirit that reechoes the very morals and principles of the students of a school. It is the spirit of justice and fair play, the unrequited practice of honesty, the ever striving for service to others. This and this alone is the spirit that is in reality worth while. It is for this standard that we should and are striving. It is not the cigarette fiend, that from the bleachers continually puffs one after another, who claims that so much is his love for his school that he bets all that he has and waves a small wad of one dollar bills around in the air, that constitutes a worth while student body. Rather it is the one whom the boys call "book worm", who leaves the campus late after a hard day's study with a scholarship medal on his watch chain, or the athlete who after dark is reaching home after a stiff work-out; it is this element that represents the high ideals of a school, and above all it is this element that carries a worth while school spirit with him out into the world. And this is where school spirit first begins to show itself. It is not his class room recitation that determines the salary of a man, but what he carries with him to the office. Likewise it is not the air which is manifested on the campus that proclaims manliness and loyalty to your school, but your actions toward your fellow men in the world.

We have our campus spirit, but we must carry this spirit on with us. Remember that the world is a large school preparing for the great eternity which is to follow. And as we enter life's arena let us stick fast to that old traditional spirit of loyalty, fairness, honesty and service, and bury deep in the walls of our hearts the old motto that has so oft inspired us and contributed largely to our present success, "Where only the best is good enough."

—*R. C. H.*

STRIVE AND SUCCEED

Seniors: Has our high school course meant what it should mean to us? Together with the book knowledge, have we learned some lesson that is going to stay with us through life? Some lesson of truth, or perhaps love?

The time has come for us to think of ourselves not as girls and boys who leave all their vital problems for their parents to solve for them; because we are making our own future and if we lag behind we must account for it ourselves. After we leave high school we are no longer that care-free, youthful, happy band that people have looked upon with admiration. We are now starting out on the long voyage of life. Will it be a worth while one? It will be if we make it what we should. Have we the true Christian heart that it takes for a person to make friends—friends that will last? If we have health, knowledge, ambition and youth, with all of its inspiring imagination and do not have a dependable nature, and a true, unselfish heart that enjoys only the things that are upright and excellent, we can never expect to reach that glorious goal, Success. But can we succeed in this life by simply being honest, true and unselfish to our fellowmen? No, we must labor, we must deny ourselves things that we know will bring us mere worldly pleasure. The harder we work for a thing, the better it will seem in the end when we have attained it. We must learn to depend on ourselves for everything and not leave it to the other fellow; things that we work out for ourselves will always stay with us, but learning what the other fellow has originated will not teach us the same lesson.

When talking it is not best to be too conscious of oneself: but it is wise for us to think long before we do an act that is going to cause the public to criticise—whether it be good or bad criticism. The public judges us every day and now is the time when they're summing us up to see if we are strong enough to become leaders in our churches, educational enterprises, homes, and businesses. It is all life, and every day we are determining our future—whether we call it luck or fate. Slowly the strong and worthy are surpassing the weak and unworthy.

Which side will we be on in the end? All of us have ambitious minds, why not set our goal now and work to that end?

Let us as the Senior class of '24 resolve in our minds this day that we will try to live up to our motto—*"Strive and Succeed."*

—*D. D.*

LOOKING FORWARD

"For I dipt into the future, far as human eye could see,
Saw the vision of the world, and all the wonder that would be."

We experience at this time a sweet feeling of sadness at the "parting of the ways," as we leave behind the place of our many happy days, and our occasional sorrowful ones. But this should not be the main note in our song. As we receive our diplomas we stop to think about the name given to the ceremony—Commencement; surely a name not meant to make us look backward to our school days, but forward to what is largely in our own hands.

At present all of us are looking forward to something with more or less keen speculation. Those of us who are so fortunate as to graduate this year are looking ahead to attending college or starting in now to realize on the investment already made in education by obtaining a position. Others are expecting either to keep up the good work of education or to drop out without finishing the course.

But what do we see in the distant future, when we shall be looking back on our high school and college days? Shall we look back with regret for failing to live up to our expectations, or shall we feel that we have succeeded in our purpose? The answer lies largely in the goal which we set before ourselves, whether it be to acquire wealth and social position, to be prosperous in the business world, or simply to find happiness.

When we reach that age, which now seems so vague and uncertain, we may have attained all of the above-mentioned goals; if so, we shall be extremely fortunate. But the first two, and as many more as we can add, will be entirely empty and void unless accompanied by the last. For what is success? It is "the prosperous termination of any enterprise," to use the words of the dictionary. Clearly, then, the degree of the attained success is governed largely by the height of the goal which we set out to win.

We should set our mark so high that we may never fully realize success; yet in striving toward that end we may accomplish much for the benefit of mankind.

"Hitch your wagon to a star,
Keep your seat—and there you are."

—*G. C. H.*

LIBRARY

Our Library

It is not our purpose as we close this, another very successful school year, to magnify in your minds the library, and neither would we have you for a moment think too much of this one phase of our life and forget the other departments which have contributed much to our success. If we should look about to find which department had touched the most students and been profitable to each of the one thousand and ten now enrolled in the school, we would be forced to place the library in that coveted place. In closing this year it is proper that we stop and learn a few facts about the library and at the same time arrive at some estimate of its value. Many are the daily visitors in the library but they are ignorant of the great educational value this part of our progressive educational system carries with it. Even those who use its advantages most do not understand how tremendous is its work and its possibilities.

We are proud to say that the same spirit which gave the Richard J. Reynolds Memorial High School this library is causing its growth, and instead of 2300 books we today have 3657. Out of the 148 days our library was open 62,867 students paid it a visit and over 12,000 books were taken out for home use. The average daily attendance would total nearly 500, or about half of our present enrollment. During the year fines to the amount of $28.10 were collected. Aside from the fact that many books are used for recreational reading much required reference reading is done in the library also. Over 1,000 books were placed on the reference shelf and as we look back we wonder how we progressed under our old system, and it brings a new appreciation of the library and its possibilities. The above facts date to May 1, but here we get an insight into the great number of students touched and its tremendous circulation.

The library is by no means complete and each year will find new improvements and a more efficient library for the use of the students of this high school. Many of us are seniors and some will leave this institution to resume their studies in higher branches of education, while others will enter life as products of this institution, but the real worth of the library will always linger in their minds and when they visit similiar institutions the memory of the library —will be renewed and they will be proud of the nucleus of this great educational system which has done so much for them. May the under classmen realize the possibilities at hand and use the library in the coming years as never before.

In passing it would be proper to mention the pages who have assisted Mrs. Koos in the library work this year. There were sixteen in all, and to them is due much credit for increasing the efficiency of

ORCHESTRA

the library and making it possible for Mrs. Koos to attend to the individual needs of the students.

Through these facts presented you have seen the significance of our library and the work done during the past year. Its success could not have been greater. There is a reason for every success and the praise for the success of the library must go to Mrs. Koos, our librarian. Through her untiring efforts and her kind, courteous, sympathetic service each student has come to love the library; we are not only proud of our library, but we are proud of Mrs. Koos, Miss Moore, Miss Thompson, and any of the other faculty members who have made it such a success.

—*Hanselle L. Hester*

Music Work of the Past Year

W.-S. H. S. is now winning cups in the art of music. It has long been her custom to take cups in athletics, typewriting, declamation and debate work, etc., and she now has won another cup by possessing the best and most complete orchestra in the state.

The contest was held in Greensboro, N. C., Friday night, May 2, 1924. It was a big event, including instrumental and vocal solos, vocal quartettes, choruses, glee clubs, and then the orchestral contest. The result in the orchestral contest was: Winston-Salem, first; Roanoke Rapids, second.

It was not an overwhelming victory, however, for the other schools had wonderful orchestras as well. Roanoke Rapids, especially, had a fine orchestra and must be complimented for its music. It was only in the fine points of music that the judge, Mr. George H. Gartlan, director of music in Greater New York, could make the distinction and award us the cup. Now that we have it, our director, Mr. Kutschinski, and the students composing the orchestra must be complimented for the work which they have done during the year.

Regardless of who won the prize, it is good to note that North Carolina as a whole is taking a greater interest in music and other arts than ever before.

The orchestra has not had a chance at regular playing this year because there was no place for the student body to gather. However, it has done some outside playing at banquets, etc.

The band has not been so well organized as the orchestra. Mr. Searight has held rehearsals every day but it was chiefly in preparation for next year.

Another musical organization is the Girls' Glee Club. It has been having regular practice under Mr. Searight and has developed

BAND

some good singing. The club took part in the Glee Club contest at Greensboro, but it lost.

Mr. Searight organized a Boys' Glee Club with the expectation of entering it in the contest, but a sufficient number of boys could not be gotten together and the plans were abandoned. However, Mr. Searight got a quartette from them, but owing to a lack of time they could not get the necessary songs ready for the contest.

Although only one cup has been won in music, much preparation has been made for next year and the various musical organizations expect to take all trophies as well as give every student a chance to learn something about music.

—R. F.

R. J. REYNOLDS (WINSTON-SALEM) HIGH SCHOOL ORCHESTRA

C. D. KUTSCHINSKI, *Director*

FIRST VIOLIN—Edward Mickey, Archie Spaugh, Frances Hahn, Josephine Thomas, Mamie Hegwood, Marguerite Sailor, Laura Price, Esther Pfaff, Ethel Lashmit, Marjorie Tise.

SECOND VIOLIN—Jacob Sosnik, Spruill Thornton, Edward Tesh, Hanes Ellis, Maurine Langley, Mary Blue, Josephine McManus, Mary Yarborough, Clara Litteral, Jack Parrish, Livey Copple.

VIOLA—Howard Bagwell, Elizabeth Graham, Louisa Hartness, Alice Barton.

'CELLO—Katherine Hine, Kenneth Pfohl, Mary Sue Martin, Claud Swaim.

STRING BASS—Richard Pfohl, Daniel Luckenbach.

HARP—Frances Fletcher.

FLUTES—M. W. Norfleet, Jr., J. L. Johnson, Jr.

OBOES—Allie Blum, Jack Thompson, Reginald Marshall.

BASSOONS—Philip Roessel, Spencer Plaster.

CLARINETS—Edwin Stockton, Katherine Pfohl, Harvey Brown, Harold Lashmit.

BARITONE SAXOPHONE—Lindsay Crutchfield.

TRUMPETS—Robert Foltz, Fred Pfaff, Odell Reich.

TROMBONES—Fred Kurtz, Norman Miller.

MELOPHONES—Fries Shaffner, Robert Barton, Coman Craver.

TUBA—Francis Wurreschke.

PERCUSSION

TYMPANI, ETC.—Stephen Morrisett.

SIDE DRUM—Earl Stryker.

BASS DRUM—Hyman Schachtman.

BLACK AND GOLD STAFF

PERSONNEL OF THE
RICHARD J. REYNOLDS HIGH SCHOOL BAND

CHRISTIAN D. KUTSCHINSKI, *Director*

ROLAND SEARIGHT, *Assistant Director*

PICCOLO—M. W. Norfleet, Jr.

FLUTE—J. L. Johnson, Jr.

E. FLAT CLARINET—Miller Wray.

SOLO B FLAT CLARINET — Edwin Stockton, Hyman Schachtman, Harold Lashmit.

FIRST B FLAT CLARINET—Harvey Brown, Katherine Pfohl, Murice Talley.

SECOND B FLAT CLARINET—Hunter Phillips, Earl Stryker, Hubert Rayhill.

THIRD B FLAT CLARINET—Joe Cude, Walter White, David Embler.

OBOE—Reginald Marshall, Allie Blum, Jack Thompson.

BASSOON—Philip Roessel, Spencer Plaster.

SOPRANO SAXOPHONE—Dwight Linville, Dorsey P. Stimson.

ALTO SAXOPHONE—Dana Jester, Ned Heefner.

TENOR SAXOPHONE—Wm. Ford, Allen Biles.

C MELODY SAXOPHONE—James Dodson, Wm. Chandler, Jack White.

BARITONE SAXOPHONE—Lindsay Crutchfield.

SOLO Bb CORNET—Robert Foltz, Fred Pfaff, Odell Reich, Charles Moester.

FIRST Bb CORNET—Howard Burgin, James Harper, Everett Snyder, John Barnes.

SECOND Bb CORNET—David Wurreschke, Clement Chambers, Henry Trotter, Claud Land.

THIRD Bb CORNET—Clyde Holder, Wm. McGehee, Ralph Blalock, George Turner.

FIRST Eb ALTO—Fries Shaffner, Robert Barton.

SECOND Eb ALTO—Coman Craver, John Brindle.

THIRD Eb ALTO—Worth Newsome.

FOURTH Eb ALTO—Homer McCann.

FIRST TROMBONE—Fred Kurtz, Norman Miller.

SECOND TROMBONE—Archie Spaugh.

THIRD TROMBONE—Theron Walsh.

BARITONE—Kenneth Pfohl, Daniel Luckenbach, Odell Craver, Conrad Southern.

BASS AND TUBA—Francis Wurreschke, Richard Pfohl, Ralph Frazier.

DRUMS—Howard Bagwell, Edward Mickey, Stephen Morrisett.

DEBATING TEAM

The Aycock Debate

Another year has brought with it another Aycock Debating Contest, and again we entered the fray not only with firm determination and high hopes but with the quality of debaters that enabled us to be justified in our feeling of safety. And we have emerged from this "battle of the wits" without disappointment, knowing that the best effort was expended on the part of our teams and that the goal was not far off.

This year the Aycock Triangular Debates were conducted as usual, each negative team journeyed over to debate the affirmatives on the home territories. Our triangle is composed of Asheville, Greensboro, and Winston-Salem. This year our negative debated Greensboro's affirmative in Greensboro while Asheville's negative debated our affirmative here. The query for discussion this year was, Resolved: That the Inter-Allied War Debt Should Be Canceled.

The great clash over the whole of North Carolina came on the night of March 28. Our affirmative team, consisting of Charles Hamilton and Hanselle Hester, was awarded the decision. The contest was one of unusual interest, but the opposition was no match for the well prepared home team. However, our negative team, composed of Joe Carlton and Richard Horne, was not so fortunate. They made a splendid showing in Greensboro and presented many keen arguments. But the Greensboro team was chosen the winner by the judges. The rules of the contest are that both teams must win out to compete at Chapel Hill, so Winston-Salem was dropped from further contest. However, our spirits are not crushed by our defeat.

We are indeed glad that we have had the opportunity of participating in this debate and have done so with credit. We are sure that we have lost nothing but gained much. It is our desire to continue in these competitions and with the splendid material in prospect we can next year once more go forth to war with banners flying high and a well directed fire.

—B. E.

Declamation

The old Black and Gold closes a very successful year in the art of declaiming. Not only have we faithfully participated in all the declamation contests offered in the state but we have had the good fortune in at least one instance to return a winner. Of course it must not be construed that the crown of success was our primary purpose, but to derive the most good out of an undertaking one must strive the hard-

TYPEWRITING TEAM

est. The prize is only a token or symbol of excellence through hard work.

We were represented in four contests. The first was at Emory and Henry College, Virginia. Our representative was Hanselle Hester, who made a good appearance, and entered the final. He was unsuccessful there, however.

Following this contest was the State-wide Declamation Contest at Wake Forest, April 4. Ben Eaton representing us there came through as winner of the third place and was awarded a bronze medal. There were forty-six schools participating and the contest was not without excitement.

The Trinity Contest was the next in order. Joe Carlton was chosen as our representative. On April 18, with thirty-six contesting, Joe was awarded the beautiful gold medal given by the 9019 Society. The school cherishes his success and claims it as her own.

On April 26 Joe Carlton also appeared in the State-wide Declamation Contest at Guilford. Like the others this contest did not lack for keen competition among the speakers. Joe was successful in the preliminaries, but lost in the final round.

The declamation contests we can conscientiously say have been well worth our attention. These contests have all been of a high type. They are not only valuable to those entering but to the school itself; for a victory or even mere representation means a source of real advertisement for the school.

We are indeed proud of our school's representation this year and welcome the opportunity for a return of these contests next year.

—*B. E.*

The Typewriting Contest

Regardless of the fact that the second-year typewriting team made an average of seven and two-thirds more words per minute than that of last year we came out third in the state contest held May 3rd at the new North School.

The second-year team was composed of Lena West, Doris Cox, Sam Buie, Ralph Choplin, Henry Heitman, Allie Hege, and Hanes Carter. The three who made the highest average of our team were: Henry Heitman 57, Ralph Choplin 55, Lena West 54. According to the rules of the state contest the average of the three highest members gives the team average, which was 55 2/3 for our team.

The contest held this year was the closest that has ever been held. Raleigh won over Charlotte by two-thirds of a word and over our team by just one word. For seven successive years we have brought

HI-Y CLUB

home the honors offered in this contest, winning two cups and having
. the third one for a`year.,

    --- Louise Yarbrough made the second highest average in the first-
year contest with a net average of forty-five words per minute. The
other members of the team were: Ambler Major 42, Franklin Mat-
thews 43.

    Miss Margaret Neely won the honor of being the state champion
typist with an average of seventy-nine words a minute for fifteen
minutes.

    The one-minute contest was won by Miss Hazel Ferguson, who
wrote ninety-seven words in one minute making only one error.

    The members of the Black and Gold teams and all students of
the typewriting classes feel greatly indebted to their efficient teacher,
Miss Josephine Wilson, who has worked so faithfully and patiently
in making the teams what they are today. In spite of the fact that we
did not win the state championship we have the joy of knowing that
she has raised the standard higher by seven points than that of last
year. The members of the first-year team have declared that they are
going to do their very best to win the cup next year and unless Raleigh
puts out an unusually good team the cup will be coming back to
Winston-Salem next spring.

                                                    —*M. H.*

The Hi-Y

    Much was expected of the Hi-Y Clubs this year under the
"three club idea"—Sophomore, Junior, Senior—which was successfully started last year. All expectations were very satisfactorily ful-
filled, for the clubs as a whole enjoyed a very successful year under
the excellent supervision of Mr. Alton C. Roberts, Boys' Work
. Secretary of the Y. M. C. A., and the faithful service of the following
officers of the various clubs:

    Senior—Owen Chatham, President; John Foster, Vice-President;
Newton Ebaugh, Secretary; Edwin Stockton, Treasurer.

    Junior—Robert Hatcher, President; Joe Carlton, Vice-Presi-
dent; James Crawford, Secretary; J. J. Gentry, Treasurer.

    Sophomore—Durant Pinkston, President; Norman Miller, Vice-
President; Ned Heefner, Secretary and Treasurer.

    The Senior club has a membership of twenty-four, the Junior
club a membership of nineteen, and the Sophomore club a membership
of thirteen. The faculty advisors of the Senior, Junior and Sophomore clubs, respectively, are Mr. McNew, Mr. C. H. Rollins
and Mr. Dick.

    Each week the three clubs meet together for supper at the Y. M.

C. A. Here the members of the different clubs are brought closer together in clean fellowship and made to feel that each is a part of a unit working for the welfare of the boys in the high school. Immediately after the supper the clubs retire to separate rooms and there a very helpful half-hour is spent in Bible study and different courses are adopted by each club. The Seniors, under the leadership of Mr. D. L. Rights, are studying the "High Calling"; the Juniors, under Mr. C. H. Rollins, are studying a general course dealing with problems of every-day life and school interests; the Sophomores, under Mr. Donald Van Noppen, are studying "Life Problems and Bible Discussions for High School Boys."

Many activities have been undertaken by the clubs as a unit, one of the most important being that of the organization of the F-Y Club, which is composed of boys from the Freshman class and having the same ideals and principles upon which the Hi-Y clubs are operated. The boys entered very enthusiastically upon the task of soliciting delegates to the Older Boys' Conference in Greensboro. A large number of the boys went around to the various churches and spoke in behalf of the conference and after a very successful campaign it was found that eighty delegates were secured—the largest delegation ever sent to such a conference from Winston-Salem. By vote the clubs decided to help in the membership contest put on by the Y. M. C. A., and after a very successful effort by the members the F-Y Club won the contest by soliciting more members than any other organization.

The social phase of the Hi-Y Program was most effectively carried out in the most enjoyable events of the Christmas Banquet with an attendance of sixty, and the April party with an attendance of sixty-eight. These events were much enjoyed and voted a decided success by each member present. There will probably be a picnic at the close of the year which will wind up the year's program.

On the whole the feeling is that this year has been a most successful one for the Hi-Y clubs in furthering the club purpose, which is "to create, maintain and extend thruout the school and community high standards of Christian character." Along with this purpose the members of the club have tried to maintain the school spirit and carry out the slogan of clean living, clean scholarship and contagious Christian character.

—*J. F.*

9L2 Holds a Democratic Convention

Who says that women know nothing about politics? Certainly no one who attended the 9L2 political convention would dare make such a statement. For, under the able direction of Miss McDowell, the class was transformed into an important assembly of politicians, met for the purpose of selecting the Democratic nominee for the presidency of the United States.

Five promising candidates were chosen for the race. They were: Oscar Underwood—Ida Hatcher; Al Smith—Lucile Norman; Royal Copeland—Edith Perryman; William Gibbs McAdoo—Loretta Carroll; Mr. Ralston—Mell Efird. Each of the gentlemen selected a campaign manager—and the fight was on!

For days before election the blackboards were plastered with glaring notices to the public and sundry entreaties and exhortations to vote for certain candidates.

On May 5, 1924, the convention assembled together with Miss Moore's history class, which had been invited. Several distinguished guests were present, among them Miss Mebane, Miss Northrop, Miss Martin, and Miss Moore. These visitors modestly seated themselves at the back of the room and allowed the candidates to monopolize the limelight. Miss Katherine Boyles acted as chairman and opened the meeting with an inspiring address, urging the members to vote for the very best man. Oscar Underwood then stated his platform in a rousing speech, supported by his campaign manager, Fritz Firey, who declared him to be the "White Hope of the South." Al Smith and his campaign manager, Lucile Vest, came next and fought hard for anti-prohibition. Mr. Copeland followed these with his manager, Laila Wright, who asserted that "Doc" Copeland "could cure the ills of the government without giving oil." After these came McAdoo and his campaign manager, Rebecca Landquist, who urged the delegates to vote for McAdoo "who clears today of past regret and future fears." Last came Ralston, who stated his platform with remarkable eloquence. He was supported by his manager, Eloise Vaughan.

A vote was then taken and Oscar W. Underwood (Ida Hatcher) received the highest number of votes, having more than all the rest of the candidates together. McAdoo and Ralston received the next highest number.

After a few words from the chairman, who congratulated the candidates for their extraordinary oratorical skill, the convention adjourned and all delegates hastened to further congratulate Mr. Underwood, the Democratic nominee for the presidency.

—L. C.

MONOGRAM CLUB

The Monogram Club

The Monogram Club has been in existence for four years and many of the high school leaders have come from its ranks. The twenty-four members are among the school's athletic leaders, since only letter-men for football, tennis, baseball, basketball or track are eligible for membership. The purpose of the club is an admirable one, for it seeks to instill into its members a more lofty school spirit and a deeper fellowship among themselves.

The present officers of the Monogram Club are: Robert Hatcher, president; Robah Veach, vice-president, and Ralph Frazier, secretary and treasurer. Conspicuous among former presidents have been Miles Davis and Leo Caldwell. The athletic coaches are honorary members and serve as the club advisors. They are: Mr. Leonard Dick, football and track coach; Mr. Courtney Kesler, assistant football coach; Mr. C. R. Joyner, baseball coach; Mr. Jefferson Johnson, assistant baseball coach; Mr. Hathaway, basketball coach. The club owes much of its success and popularity to these supervisors and the enthusiasm of the club officers.

The club has been especially active this year. Public attention was first drawn to its initiation ceremonies, which were decidedly unique. An interesting feature was the parade, which called forth much favorable comment.

The Monogram Minstrel, given by the club this spring, will go down in high school history as one of the most successful affairs of the school year. Its popularity was due to the loyal efforts of the faculty as well as the cooperation and enthusiasm of the club members. By popular request the minstrel was repeated recently in the fine new auditorium. The club has decided to make such an entertainment an annual event. The profits will be used to erect full length portraits of Leo Caldwell and George Stanley. A sick fund, for the purpose of paying the hospital expenses of all boys injured on the athletic field, will also be established. From the remaining funds tiny gold emblems will be purchased for each member, signifying the sport in which he majors. These are to be presented at the closing exercises of the school.

The Monogram Club is an organization to which any high school letter-man may consider it a privilege to belong. It is one of the really important groups that foster school spirit and contribute so much to the unit of high school life.

—L. C.

FOOT BALL TEAM

Football is coming to be one of the greatest, if not the greatest form of high school and college athletics. It is by far the most popular. This popularity of the game is due to the fact that there is always variety in the game. When a man has seen one game, he has not seen all there is to be seen; he has only begun his football education. There are always new plays to be seen, and new developments under different circumstances in the old standard plays. Because of this variety of the game, and the fact that the American public craves violent action, football is fast becoming a most popular game.

Because of its educational, mental, and physical developing value, and because of the school spirit which it creates, the Winston-Salem High School has always backed this game, in conjunction with all other forms of constructive athletics, to the limit.

Our past football season was successful, so far as winning games, creating school spirit, and mental and physical development was concerned; but the tragedy which ended our season will always be remembered by the team-mates and class-mates of Leo Caldwell.

The results of the games were as follows:

Winston-Salem	25		Durham	0
Winston-Salem	9		Greensboro	0
Winston-Salem	45		Spencer	7
Winston-Salem	3	(3rd quarter)	Charlotte	0

HOCKEY TEAM

Hockey

The local high school blazed a new trail in sports when the girls began playing hockey in the fall for the first time. So far as is known we have the honor of being the first high school in the South to play this interesting and fascinating outdoor game. Pretty soon after we began to play, the high school at Southern Pines started. Leaksville expressed a desire to begin in the spring.

Hockey is a game that requires quick thought and action, and is the fastest sport offered for girls. It has been played successfully in the various colleges for a number of years, while quite a few high schools in the North and Middle West now include it in their major sports for girls.

The line-up and position is the same as football, with eleven players on each side. There are two inside forwards, one center forward, two outside forwards (better known as wings), three half-backs, two full-backs, and the goal keeper.

When the game begins a ball about the size of a baseball, but hard like a golf ball, is brought to the center of the field and bullied off. This ball is knocked with sticks shaped like a golf stick but larger and made entirely of wood. The stick has a round side and a flat side; the ball must be hit with the flat side or it is a foul. The object is to get the ball through the goal post at the opposite end of the field while the players on that side are trying to keep it away from the goal and going in the other direction toward their goal. Each time the ball goes through the goal posts it counts one point.

To people who do not know the rules of hockey or how it is played it all seems like a compound-complex puzzle, but it is really not complicated. Although a long hard stroke may be used to good advantage at times, the player who can dribble the ball and make short accurate strokes is usually the most valuable player. When making a hard stroke the player often raises the stick over the shoulder to give more force to the stroke, and this is a foul.

We were unable to play any outside games in the fall but our efficient coach, Miss Summerell, hopes to be able to schedule some for next year. The varsity team at N. C. C. W. planned to play a picked team from here just before Christmas, but the game had to be canceled because of the heavy rains.

A game was played by the local girls National Field Day that called forth much favorable comment.

Hockey is now included in the major sports for girls, having been added at the last State meeting. Points will now be awarded for a school letter as in any other major sport.

—*Mamie Hegwood '25*

BOYS' BASKETBALL TEAM

BASKETBALL

The cage game is another form of athletic training which is offered in our high school. This game is always popular because of the merits of the game itself, and the fact that in mid-winter we have no other sports to divert our attention.

Basketball has always been well backed up in Winston High School, both by students and teachers turning out for the games, and by efficient players trying out for the team.

The past season of the Black and Gold warriors was not quite up to standard. The basketballers got off to a bad start, but although it took them some time to get back into old time form, they played several good games; the hardest game of the season being with Greensboro, in which Greensboro won in the last minute of play.

The reason for our weakened condition was that we had an abundance of new material; and although the season was not so successful in games won, it was a season profitably spent, for with this year's experience under the efficient coaching of Mr. L. B. Hathaway, the lads will play like veterans next year.

The players as they appear in the picture are, left to right—Top row—Ford, Houchins, Petree, Plaster, Lentz, Joyner (manager); Second row—Roan, G. Hatcher, Cofer (captain), Johnson, Watkins.

—O. C.

GIRLS' BASKETBALL TEAM

GIRLS' BASKETBALL

Basketball season is over, and even though our girls did not bring back the championship, as they did last year, we are proud of them just the same. The members of the team as well as the coaches worked hard and they certainly deserve credit.

Our first game was with Greensboro, at Greensboro, and we lost with a score of 5—23. Our next game was with Reidsville, at Reidsville. This time we were the winners by 20—14. Then we went to High Point and carried away the victory there by 38—13. After playing Leaksville and Thomasville we began our championship games, the first of which was with South Buffalo at Guilford College on March 14. This was the first game we had ever played with South Buffalo, and we did not know what to expect. But we found them comparatively easy and won the day by a great big score, 28—6. But on March 7 again on neutral grounds at Guilford College, we met our "Waterloo." Greensboro, our old enemy, proved a little too much for even our spunky girls. Games may come and games may go, but there never will be another game like that one. Each side was determined to win and each side fought. The score went up one point at a time, first in favor of Winston, then in favor of Greensboro. Each team put up a stiff fight, but in the last half of the last quarter Greensboro made a goal, raising the tie 17—17 to 17—19. We were unable to score again so Greensboro won the day. It was not an easy victory for them, however, for our team stood its ground and fought a good fight.

The games of the season are as follows:

Winston-Salem	5	vs.	Greensboro	23
"	20	vs.	Reidsville	14
"	28	vs.	High Point	13
"	14	vs.	Leaksville	17
"	30	vs.	Thomasville	6
"	19	vs.	Leaksville	17
"	12	vs.	High Point	12
	18	vs.	Greensboro	30
		(Championship games)		
"	28	vs.	South Buffalo	6
"	17	vs.	Greensboro	19

The Varsity line-up was as follows:

Pet Sheppard, (Captain); Lillian Cromer, (Guard); Moselle Stephenson, (Guard); Laeke Lentz, (Forward); Maye Simpson (Forward); Susie Weatherman, (Forward).

—*T. R.*

BOYS' BASEBALL TEAM

The "rah-rahs" from the bleachers have stopped. The baseball suits are folded up and packed away until next year. The prints of the spiked shoes have left Hanes' field. It is now time to erect a monument to our baseball team, for it is dead until next year. Still we do not say dead, for Winston-Salem boys always have "that fighting spirit."

Nevertheless, the fact remains that W.-S. H. S. lost and in only one game. Whether it was due to the enemy finding the formula for hitting Pitcher Ernest's curved balls, we will not attempt to say. Just the same the headline remains, W.-S. 9; Thomasville, 11. In Thomasville's case it was—9, come 11.

It is hard to explain how Thomasville, the first one on the championship series, beat us other than by saying it had the better team. Up to that time our team was tootin' its own horn, having won 5 out of 8 games by good scores; in other words, they weren't expected to stop so suddenly. The Thomasville High simply had a good team.

Baseball prospects at the first of the season were very good. Everyone was a heavy hitter. It is told that Sapp, when at High Point, knocked one so far that High Point had to send after it by an airplane. As I was not there, I cannot vouch for the authenticity of that story. With either Ernest or Ford in the box and Sapp behind the plate, the batter had to be a good one to get a hit of any value.

The team didn't lack basemen or fielders either, for they had

GIRLS' BASEBALL TEAM

Finlator, Watkins, Cofer, Hatcher and all the other little boys scattered out there. So the line-up was as strong as the Hindenburg line until the Thomasville bomb landed in its midst.

The team will lose very few of its valuable men for next year, Sapp being, probably, the only one who will leave. With the old men and new material and Coach Joyner's wise direction the next year's team should make as good a showing as any.

Winston-Salem	8	Mt. Airy	4
"	6	High Point	5
"	8	High Point	5
	2	Spencer	3
"	7	Greensboro	0
"	2	Thomasville	10
"	9	Spencer	4
	4	Trinity	11
	9	*Thomasville	11
"	20	Trinity	14

*(Championship)

—R. F.

GIRLS' BASEBALL

The girls of our Athletic Association have a new sport—girls' baseball. We're young yet, but give us time and we will show you how we can uphold the fine spirit and playing of the other athletic teams.

The team was organized early in April by Miss Smith, and interest was easily aroused. Practices have been held regularly on Tuesdays and Fridays since that time. More students have attended these practices than the practices of any other sport this year.

As soon as the teams could be chosen several inter-class games were played. The teams were backed by great interest and enthusiasm from the other students.

On Friday, May 2, our team played the Greensboro High School team of Greensboro. Although we were defeated we are not discouraged but look forward to being victorious in the future.

The following compose the Winston-Salem girls' baseball team: Maye Simpson, Laeke Lentz, Ruth Anthony, Frances Chandler, Doris Lentz, Lucile Lee, Mary Anthony, Mildred Russ, Davie Bell Eaton, Aurelia Plumly, Ruth Carter, Elizabeth Hines.

All on the baseball team are worthy of praise and we are looking forward to seeing baseball continue as it has begun. We hope to see next year's team uphold the same spirit and interest which has been shown this season.

—*Elizabeth Hines, '25*·

BOYS' TRACK TEAM

TRACK

With only one loving cup decorating our path of success in track this year, we feel that our track men are heroes on the field and veterans of many hard fought battles. Surely it would do justice to neither the team and the coach, who have labored so diligently, nor to the school at large, to measure our success in material terms. We, having been winners of the benefits of every meet, are not able to offer any panacea; however, justice to all concerned necessitates a few cold facts. The first is, we have not had the teaching, for though we possess the best coach in the state we have not complied with that age-old law of Plato, "practice makes perfect". In cold facts, we have met our fellow schools on the field for but two years, including this present one. Thus we see that we are babies at the game and cannot expect the returns of our professional neighbors. The other fact, even more vital than the former, is that we have not had a track on which to practice. This handicap has nipped in the bud the success of our team.

We entered three state track meets, one at Carolina, one at Guilford College and the last at Greensboro. At the University the reliable Houchins scored second in the broad jump and Ford came in third in the half mile. From this meet we amassed only five points. At Guilford we made a much better showing. We won first in the mile-relay, thus getting a silver loving cup. Cofer came in

GIRLS' TRACK TEAM

second in the two-twenty; Houchins scored second in the broad jump, and third in the one-hundred; and Newman was third in the discus. From this meet we amassed a total of sixteen points, won fourth place, and in reality should have been second according to new rules which Guilford has not yet adopted. Frazier knocked over both the first and last hurdle; this, according to Guilford's rules, eliminated him, though with this year's new track rules a man is allowed to knock over two hurdles, both of which may be the first and last. We are well satisfied with the returns of this meet. The accident that practically eliminated us from the third meet was the fact that Houchins sprained his ankle. At Greensboro we made a creditable show. Frazier came in second in the hurdles in good time, 16:1; Cofer was third in the two-twenty, Houchins third in the broad and Newman fourth in the discus. This was a very spectacular meet in which five high school records are known to have been broken. From this meet we totaled twelve points and fifth place.

Our prospects for next year seem exceptionally good. We lose only one varsity man, Bolich, to Trinity. In less than three weeks we shall have completed on the campus the finest track in North Carolina. With this material and the prospects for the return of such an able man as Coach Dick, who has been the very backbone of this year's success, nothing should be able to stop us. Surely the least we have to look forward to is not only the fastest track team in North Carolina, but also the one with the best fighting spirit.

—*R. C. H.*

GIRLS' TRACK

"Get on your mark; get set; go," could be heard every afternoon during the training season, as Miss Summerell trained our track team for the athletic meet.

In spite of the fact that a number of the practices could not be held on account of the rain and mud, the local team made a splendid showing at the District Field Meet held in Greensboro.

Members of the upper classes were too busy with their studies to come out for track, but the freshmen "stuck fast." When it came time to show up for the Black and Gold they were right there.

Frances Chandler won first place for us in the 50-yard dash. Doris Lentz won third place.

Lillian Jarvis and Leona Heathe won second and third places, respectively, in the 75-yard dash.

Doris Lentz called forth all kinds of exclamations when she gave her usual swing and jumped over 26 feet in the hop-step-jump contest. She won second place, but she was much handicapped by the size of the other girls who were in the contest.

GIRLS' TENNIS TEAM

The potato relay race was won by the local team. Each girl had the circle and swing that brought our team in about two players ahead. We came out third in the baseball speed relay. One of the girls hung to the hoop used in the color relay just a bit too long, and the team came out third.

When it came time to don trousers, vest and hat, and walk the rail with an open umbrella and a traveling bag they just took too much time. Some of the girls had to take time to push their locks under their caps, and they would have used a mirror if they could have found one.

Our team won third place in total points. In the field events High Point scored 29 points, Greensboro 22, and Winston-Salem 20, while South Buffalo had 12.

Now that Hanes Field is being put into first-class shape the girls will not be handicapped for a place to practice next year. The field will be well drained and will not be so muddy as it was this year.

The team was composed of the following: Miss Frances Summerell, coach; Mildred Russ, Etta Terrell, Doris Lentz, Frances Chandler, Leona Heathe, Margaret Mickey, Ruth Anthony, Lillian Jarvis, Alice McClennahan, Annie Hobbs, Ada Frazier, Mildred Cunningham, Martha Anthony, Adelaide Crawford and Mamie Hegwood, manager.

—*M. H.*

Girls' Tennis

This year the tennis team has done some splendid work and we expect those girls on the team who are graduating to do some good work in other fields after graduation.

Those on the team are: Alice Lamb, Cordelia Shaner—doubles; Lillian Cromer, Moselle Stephenson—singles; Josephine Huntley—substitute.

The games played so far are:
1. Winston-Salem—Leaksville, at Greensboro. Winston-Salem won.
2. Winston-Salem — Greensboro, at Greensboro. Greensboro won.
3. Winston-Salem—Greensboro, here.

In this game Moselle lost her singles. Lillian played and won. Josephine played and lost. Cordelia and Alice played doubles and won.

We are looking forward to a great success for Winston-Salem in the future games.

—*D. D.*

BOYS' TENNIS TEAM

Boys' Tennis

The Black and Gold boys' tennis team has been looking forward to a very successful year. The team that was picked by elimination consists of John Foster and Archibald Spaugh. Both are old letter-men, and are full worthy of representing our school. With John and Archie playing doubles and John playing singles our school should feel proud of its tennis team.

Our school was represented by these boys in the State championship matches at Chapel Hill, and all was going our way, until they lost to Greensboro, after a hard fight. This defeat eliminated us, but it is pleasing to note that the team that had such a hard time defeating us later won the championship.

After the championship matches at Chapel Hill, the team played in its first Inter-High School Meet with Greensboro in Greensboro. In this meet they lost their doubles match and also lost one and tied one in their single matches. But on May 6, in the return match with Greensboro, our team completely outclassed the visitors, winning the doubles and winning one and losing one of the single matches. This success shows that the team is just reaching its stride and will reflect honor on our school.

Mr. Haltiwanger, who is coach and manager of the tennis team, has many matches scheduled for the late spring, and he feels confident that his team will come through these games with winning colors.

—C. H.

Something New

One of the most successful and enjoyable social events of the school year was the dinner given by the Girls' Athletic Association this spring in the High School Cafeteria. The members of the Association and the lady members of the faculty were present.

On arriving at the school at 6:30, the guests went immediately to the Cafeteria, where places were indicated by dainty place-cards. The room was beautifully and appropriately decorated with black and gold crepe paper and gold-colored candles. Hockey sticks, tennis racquets, and baseball bats and balls were arranged in the windows, each tied with a tiny bow of black and gold paper.

A delicious three-course dinner was served to the guests during the evening. Between courses several splendid toasts were given by Maye Simpson, Adela Sheppard, and Josephine Huntley, with Moselle Stephenson, President of the Association, acting as toast-mistress. The guests were greatly favored by an interesting talk by Miss Doris Chipman, a former graduate of the High School. Miss Chipman

expressed some very interesting views on girls' athletics and her talk was greatly enjoyed by all.

One of the most interesting features of this extraordinary dinner was the chance to "see yourself as others see you." Miss Mebane had no trouble at all in recognizing herself in the person of "Lillie" Cromer, assigning the very "short lesson" of only 150 pages, and recommending "Muzzy" but especially "Mann" for references. Miss Heilig was impersonated by Jennie Lasley, who seemed very familiar with "Oui, mam'selle," and "Oh! why, my first-year class knows that." Miss Moore and also Miss Summerell could not fail to "see themselves as others see them." The most easily recognized impersonation was that of Miss Olive Smith, alias Mamie Hegwood. Miss Hegwood had obtained Miss Smith's apparel and book-bag for the occasion, making the effect very real.

For the benefit of those who were unable to attend the championsl.ip basketball game with Greensboro, the team kindly consented to go over again a few of their "striking moves." No ball was used, but none was needed. Maye Simpson once again displayed her ability and willingness to drop a ball to pick up a "down-and-outer," while Lillian Cromer and Moselle Stephenson showed how they could guard. That the audience might get the full benefit of the game, and fully realize their clever team-work, the team did their "stuff" in slow motion. After the exhibition the spectators fully understood why Greensboro had to put up such a fight to carry off the victory.

The most important event of the dinner was the reading of the list of girls who were to receive awards for "points". "Pet" Sheppard was the first to win a State Letter. The following have won such awards:

"Pet" Sheppard—State Letter and Star.
Lillian Cromer—State Letter and Star.
Josephine Huntley—Star.
Laeke Lentz—Star—State Letter.
Cordelia Shaner—Star with Letter
Moselle Stephenson—State Letter.
Martha Maslin—State Letter.
Frances Fletcher—Letter (W. H. S.).
Honorable Mention (over 100 points):
Ruth Anthony, Gwendolyn Apple, Aurelia Plumly, Susie Weatherman.

After singing a few songs together, the "good-byes" were said and each member of the Association left feeling glad she had been there.
—*T. R.*

The Black and Gold Swimming Team

Swimming, although an old form of competitive sport, is a new experiment in the High School, for this is the first year that the school has attempted to have a varsity swimming team. When the idea that the High School should have a swimming team that should compete with other schools in inter-high meets was suggested it met with the hearty approval of our citizens, the faculty and the student body.

The Y. M. C. A. at once offered the school the use of its pool, which the school gratefully accepted. Mr. Long, the physical director at the "Y", and Mr. Hathaway were selected to coach the team. The student body responded to the idea with enthusiasm and when the call for candidates for the team was made, practically every boy that could swim answered the call and began training and practicing for the coming elimination contest, which was held just before the meet with Greensboro High on May 9. In this contest the following boys were selected to represent the Black and Gold: Fred O'Brien, Newton Ebaugh, Guy Fulp, Hubert Herrin, "Bob" Blackwood, Charles Hamilton, Clarence Graham, Worth McAlister, Dana Jester, Henry Stultz, Peyton Abbott, Caldwell Roan and Henry Roan.

The first real test of the team came in the match with the Greensboro High School, which was held in the local Y. M. C. A. pool. The meet was a success in every sense of the word. The Winston boys won the match, but not until the last event had been judged. There were nine swimming events in the contest, none being too straining for high school boys and each embracing some fundamental principle of swimming. Of these events Greensboro won six first places, two second places and two third places—total points 38. Winston-Salem won three first places, seven second places and six third places—total points 39. The swimmers displayed much art and it was classed as a first-rate match. A great number of swimming fans witnessed the contest and it was seen that swimming will have a permanent place in our varsity sports.

A return match with Greensboro i now certain and other meets are pending.

—C. H.

The Best Penman in North Carolina Schools

THE grand prize for the specimen of Palmer Method writing submitted in the Fourth State-wide Contest was won for the third time by Miss Lessie Brown Phillips of the Richard J. Reynolds High School. Lessie Brown is the daughter of Mr. and Mrs. E. Roy Phillips, 199 West End Boulevard, and is an excellent student, of whom we are justly proud, for the honor is a singularly high one both for the school and the pupil.

The purpose of the contest is, "the development of greater enthusiasm and interest in the teaching and learning of better writing in the public schools of North Carolina." Mr. Bartow, of the A. N. Palmer School of Penmanship in New York City, who was judge of the contest, said that the specimens sent from Winston-Salem were much better than those of other years, and deserved special mention as the writing submitted was of an unusually high order of excellence. The work of Lessie Brown Phillips was so beautiful that he wished to reproduce it in some future number of "The Penmanship Pointer."

Especial credit should be given Pearl Longworth, a former student of Granville, who has won a prize for three successive years, and Lucile Perry, of West End, winner for the past two years.

The following pupils won prizes:

Lucile Perry, High, grade 8; Lessie Brown Phillips, High, grade 9; Pearl Longworth, High, grade 11.

Grand prize for best specimen submitted, Lessie Brown Phillips.

—Elizabeth Atkins.

Lights

The poet worships the light of the stars,
And it calls his soul from the clay
To gather the far-flung gold of the moon
Or to watch the gods at play.

The artist lives by an inner light
That casts a rosy glow
On even the sordid things of his life—
The things that no others know.

But the lights that we earthly creatures
Must love where'er we roam
Are the friendly lights in the windows
Of the places we call home.

—Loretta Carroll, '26.

Sophomore Girl Scouts

The Sophomore girls are always to be found on the field of action, for they excel in athletics. Too dignified to play with the Freshmen and too young to "hobnob" with the Juniors and Seniors, they must find an outlet for their energies. Scouting has proved a very pleasant one, and they are now enthusiastically engaged in building up a troop of girl scouts.

The entire group of about twenty-one girls is divided into three patrols of seven each. All patrols are under the direction of Miss McDowell, but each has its own officers. The patrols, their officers' names and mottoes are as follows:

Patrol I—The Ravens; motto—"Seize your opportunities"; Patrol leader, Fritz Firey; Corporal, Lucile Norman.

Patrol II—Towhee; motto—"Fly high"; Patrol leader, Adelaide Crawford; Corporal, Mary Kreeger.

Patrol III—The Humming Birds; motto — "Watch with a thousand eyes"; Patrol leader, Mell Efird; Corporal, Eloise Vaughan.

The scout motto is, "Be prepared," and that is what the Sophomore girls are striving for.

—Katherine Boyles, '26·

Experience

O winds of fate, like the winds of earth,
    Your sources none may know
And who can tell, when with bitter pow'r
    Or soft caress, you blow;
Driving men up to the noblest heights
    And dashing them down to despair;
I have been lured by your frowns and smiles,
    Found dust, and a few things fair.
O winds of life, I have borne so long
The mocking madness of your song!

I have grown brave in your cruel blast,
    Strong winds that temper and train;
Steel fingers, shaping my destiny,
    Have wrought—and not in vain.
For I have known sorrow and tasted death,
    Have thirsted, and drunk too deep
I have loved life and sought for heaven,
    And learned in my heart to keep
The spirit of your wild, sweet melody,
O winds, the echoes of eternity.

—Loretta Carroll, '26·

Intelligent Jesting

Miss Mebane: "The conditions up at the County Home are fine. The rooms are clean, the tables are covered with good things to eat."

Thelma R.: "Aw! It wasn't that way when I was up there."

Miss Mebane: "Now let us vote on who shall go to hear Lawyer Brown speak."

Henry Roan: "Miss Mebane, I want to go; my great-grandfather was a lawyer."

Senior: "I think Mr. Griffin is the most remarkable man I know."

Another S.: "Because he can get a hair cut with his hat on."

Freshman: "Mr. Herring, how old are you?"

Mr. H.: "I have seen thirty summers."

Freshman: "Mr. Herring, how many summers have you been blind?"

All joking aside, those intelligence tests really do indicate those who have brains and those who haven't—those who are absent when they are given.

Mr. Dick: "Yes, Homer Houchins won in the race."

Freshman: "I bet a yellow jacket was in his blouse."

Miss Dobson: "Mercy! What is all that noise in the hall?"

Grace Caudle: "Aw, that is Mary Crouse coming, she got the prize for the biggest feet."

Mr. Griffin: "Russell, tell me what interests you most during my talk."

Russell F. (reading a note): "Irene Byerly."

Miss Smith (to Laeke on trip): "Have you enough money to fix the car if you have trouble?"

Frances Chandler (impatient to start): "Let's go, Miss Smith. I have a dime."

One of our absent-minded teachers: "Walter, when was the treaty of—"

"Why, I'm absent today, professor," Walter interrupted.

"Oh, pardon me. Sarah, will you please answer the question?"

SAY IT WITH MUSIC

"That Red Head Gal" _____Evelyn Morris

"That Big Blond Mamma" _____Moselle Stephenson

"The Meanest Girl in Town Josephine"_____Joe Huntley

"Oh Baby" _____Peggy Brookes

"Mamma Goes Where Papa Goes"__Eleanor Franklin, Archie Spaugh

"Somebody Stole My Gal"_____Odell Sapp to 'Gene Holton

"Wonderful One" _____Harris Chamberlain

"The Sheik" _____Cooper D. Cass

"A Smile Will Go A Long, Long Way"_____Robah Veach

"They Go Wild, Simply Wild Over Me"_____Bob Hatcher

"There's Nobody Else But You"_____"Egg" Ford to Maye Tucker

"My Mann" _____Miss Mebane

"Farewell to Thee"_____Senior Class to W. H. S.

"Foolish Child" _____Bill Frazier

"Oh Gee! Oh Gosh! Oh Golly! I'm in Love"_____Cordelia Shaner

Peggy Brookes: What is your idea of a smart girl?

Odell Sapp: One who can make her complexion taste as good as it looks.

"Mine", he thought as he clasped her to him.

"I'll dig for gold here," she said to herself as she snuggled closer.

Mr. McNew (calling on Sara in Latin): Sara—Bray next.

Ask "Lilly" Cromer whose phone number 2850 is. (She will know this time).

Charles Hamilton (standing in front of his Ford when it failed to start): Just as I live in the "American Tarritories" I know why they gave you a she-name instead of a he-name. N—o—nobody but a wom—woman could be as con—contrary as you or require as much coaxing.

Mr. McNew (in Latin class): Now, girls, read between the lines and see if you can learn something you didn't know before.

"Egg": "You know more than I do."

"Pealy": "Of course I do."

"Egg": "You know me and I know you."

A slang phrase often has a deep meaning. Looking beneath its apparently meaningless grouping of words, you instantly discover an expression of clearness, consciousness and an age-old truth. There is the question asked so frequently and casually as to seem almost trivial, "What's the big idea?"

But suppose each of the graduating class of '24 asked him or herself seriously and searchingly the question. Every life depends for success and usefulness on the nature of the thought which rules it. Whether your "Big Idea" is to be an artist, a musician, a writer, a philanthropist, a merchant, a college president, or whatever it may be, it is your big idea of a profession.

Man is cowardly or heroic, worthless or useful, wretched or happy by this one test—"What is the big idea?"

When you leave the portals of the Richard J. Reynolds High School, leave with the "Big Idea" of fighting a good fight, and winning your race.

To the graduating class of '24; our sincere wishes are that life's greatest offerings come and stay with you until you have fully achieved an honorable destiny.

INQUISITIVE

George Holroyd snapped school to see the fun he would derive from it. But Mr. Moore caught him——George doesn't snap school any more.

"Monkey" Chamberlain went to see Cordelia, and rubbed "Cotton's" hair to see if he was affectionate. He wasn't.

Cooper D. Cass joined Miss Mebane's history class because he thought she was an "easy" teacher. Cooper has changed his way of thinking now.

Walter Snyder "speeded-up" to see if he could outrun the motorcycle cop. He couldn't.

The Senior Class tried to "stump" Mr. McNew on derivation of words. They couldn't.

"Rich" Horne thought that he could go in Miss Mary's class without his coat. He couldn't.

John S. Foster thought that he could read out of two Latin books at one time. He failed to accomplish the task.

HON. ROBERT F. FOLTZ, Ph. D., ORATES TO THE PHYSICS CLASS

The Physics class was fortunate enough to secure the Hon. Dr. Foltz to give a lecture on "The Value of Physics" or "The Life of a Bug." Dr. Foltz said, "A new species of horse has been developed. It is capable of carrying three people and a baby or of pulling a two-horse wagon and a Ford. Furthermore, a lightning bug has been known to give a steady light for two days. This is of great value because it is needed by miners very much. No doubt this remarkable bug will prove to be very useful for farmers to tie on their trucks while coming to the city at night."

In conclusion Dr. Foltz stated that refrigerators use ice and that lightning rods keep houses from being struck by lightning. He made the remarkable statement that mirrors reflect objects and if it were not for mirrors the fair sex of today couldn't see to powder their noses.

Dr. Foltz's speech was very enlightening, and needless to say, the Physics students know much more about this line of science than they did.

The
KIMBALL
Piano

RECOMMENDED BY MORE ARTISTS
THAN ANY OTHER PIANO

Jesse G. Bowen & Co.
526 N. Liberty St.   Phone 1882
Winston-Salem, N. C.

Miss Mebane: "Cordelia, let's have your report on Hamilton."
Cordelia: "My man is Jefferson."
(We wonder how Cordelia got the habit of saying "my man")

Mr. Moore: "Louise, Miss Wiley says you were late again this morning."
Louise J.: "That's all right, Mr. Moore. I know you are too intelligent to be influenced by what she says."

Lib S. (after finishing an arithmetic problem): "I haven't any cents left."

Lost: Senior privilege of coming in the front door. If found return immediately. Reward.

Moselle (in record shop): Have you got "Just one More Kiss?" He gave it to her.

Curtis Lane: "Those last eggs you sold me were too ripe."
Grocer: "How do you know?"
Curtis: "A little birdie told me so."

ZERO HOURS

When you break into your last dollar.
When you're called on in Latin and haven't looked at your "Jack."
When the dentist says: "It may hurt a little bit."
When you find out that your best girl has a date.
When Mr. Rollins jerks you out of the "Bread Line."
When you hear the rain and alarm clock at the same time.

DADDY GOOSE RHYMES

Hickory, dickory, dock,
The mouse ran up her sock;
But he stopped, I'm told,
For her stocking was rolled.
Hickory, dickory, dock,

CHANGEABLE MOOD

Present Tense: Ione Mebane.
Future Tense: Iona Mann.

Mr. Rollins thinks that June 8th is a "red letter day". We hope he won't change his mind.

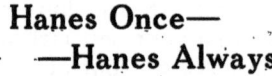

LEST WE FORGET

That Ben Eaton talks and talks and, having said nothing, says it over again.

That Eugene Holton sprained his arm patting himself on the back.

That "Steve" Sapp is the "sheik" of the Senior Class.

That Lilly Cromer can say, "Now, don't" sweeter than a baby.

That "Puppy Love" is just grand.

That Cordelia Shaner and Robah Veach are about married.

That the High School is glad that Frank Davis is leaving at last.

That "Parvus Iulius Ascanius" Holroyd and "Guisippi" Murphy are brothers.

That you are supposed to laugh at these jokes.

Bud Harper: Oh, I do wish I could sing.

Cooper D.: I do, too, if you are going to keep on trying.

Hanselle Hester: Our government has done things of which we are not exactly proud. For instance we declared war on Spain in 1898 just for killing a few million of our men.

This Issue of

𝕿𝖍𝖊 𝕭𝖑𝖆𝖈𝖐 𝖆𝖓𝖉 𝕲𝖔𝖑𝖉

Was Printed by

The Barber Printing Co.

*"Particular Printers to
Particular People"*

COMPLIMENTS OF
PIEDMONT ENGRAVING CO.

DISTINCTIVE ENGRAVINGS

WINSTON-SALEM

Charles Barton Keen
Architect

Winston-Salem, N. C.   *Philadelphia, Pa.*

*Architect for the Richard J. Reynolds
High School*

COHEN

Cohen's Smart Women's Wear

Catering especially to the
Junior and the Miss

Wear Big Winston Overalls
BIGGER---BETTER
Manufactured by

FLETCHER BROS. CO.
Wholesale Dry Goods, Notions, Clothing
Winston-Salem, N. C.

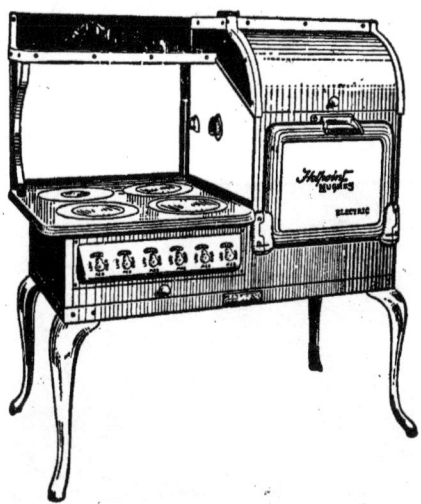

The Kitchen of Her Dreams?

It is a clean place—a bright, sunshiny room with spotless walls, and glistening utensils.

There is never the slightest trace of soot, smoke or excessive heat. Neither is there any uncertainty as to the cooking results.

It is a kitchen with an ELECTRIC RANGE.

Comfort   Economy
Dependability

Southern Public Utilities Co.

Compliments

of

American Bakeries

Company

Winston-Salem, N. C.

Herff-Jones Co.

INDIANAPOLIS

Designers and Manufacturers
of

School and College Jewelry

Jewelers to Winston-Salem High School

A Portrait

SENT TO THE ABSENT ONES NOW AND THEN, BINDS THE FRIEND-SHIPS OF YOUTH, BRIDGES DIS-TANCE AND KNITS CLOSER THE TIES OF FAMILY AND KINSFOLK.

OUR FAST LENSES, MODERN METHODS A N D EQUIPMENT, PROMPT ATTENTION AND COUR-TESY TO PATRONS HAVE MADE SITTINGS FOR PHOTOGRAPHS A REAL PLEASURE,

OUR PRICES ARE CONSISTENT WITH THE HIGH QUALITY OF OUR WORK.

Make an appointment to-day.

Ben V. Matthews

Opposite Zinzendorf Hotel

Phone 1016

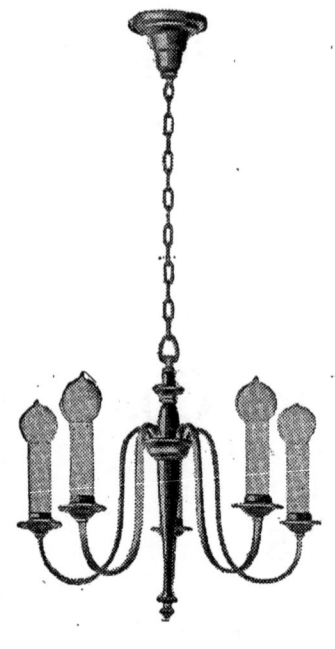